the **definitive** guide

BETTING EXCHANGES

RACING POST
expert series

3

the definitive guide to

BETTING EXCHANGES

edited by paul kealy

Raceform

Published in 2005 by Raceform Ltd
Compton, Newbury, Berkshire, RG20 6NL
Raceform Ltd is a wholly-owned subsidiary of Trinity-Mirror plc

A catalogue record for this book is available from the British Library.

ISBN 1-905153-02-3

Cover designed by Tracey Scarlett
Interiors designed by Fiona Pike

Printed by Creative Print & Design, Wales

CONTENTS

CONTRIBUTORS

PAUL KEALY joined the *Racing Post* as a racing nut in 1987, but after mixing jobs for three years, joined the Sports Betting section upon its advent in 1990. He has been there ever since and is now deputy sports editor, specialising in boxing, golf snooker and tennis.

BRUCE MILLINGTON

Bruce Millington became Sports Editor of the *The Sporting Life* in 1995 and three years later took over the same role at the *Racing Post*. He has made regular appearances on TV and radio, is the editor of *The Definitive Guide to Betting on Sport* and is regarded as one of the foremost sports betting experts in Britain.

KEVIN PULLEIN began his spectacular tipping career with *The Sporting Life* in 1994. Four years later he joined the *Racing Post* and has since established himself as the most successful football forecaster in spread betting history. His pearls of wisdom appear in his weekly Monday column, Pullein On Football, and he wrote the football betting chapter in *The Definitive Guide to Betting on Sport*.

DAVID ASHFORTH is a senior reporter and columnist with the *Racing Post*. He joined *The Sporting Life* in 1990 and, in 1998, moved to the *Racing Post*. Voted

Horserace Writer of the Year in 1996, Ashforth has written several books on social history and education, as well as horseracing. They include *Hitting the Turf, Ringers & Rascals* and *For the Good of Racing: The First 75 Years of the Tote*.

MATT WILLIAMS joined the *Racing Post* in 2000, having previously spent two years with Lambourn trainer John Hills. He soon established himself as a horseracing expert and currently produces the popular daily betting exchange section in Trading Bureau for the *Racing Post*.

PHIL AGIUS joined the *Racing Post*'s Sports Betting team in 1999 and specialises in NFL, Formula One and Non-League football.

JAMES PYMAN is the *Racing Post*'s tennis expert, whose regular Monday column, Topspin, has proved invaluable to serious tennis punters.

BETTING EXCHANGES

INTRODUCTION

By PAUL KEALY

THERE ARE THOUSANDS OF people around who have shunned the new world of betting exchanges and though they undoubtedly have their reasons, I would like to ask them a few questions.

1. Why do you think so many other punters have embraced them?

2. Why do you think Betfair has gone from nothing to arguably the largest internet betting site in the world in a few short years?

3. Why do you think bookmakers are screaming blue murder to anyone who will listen?

The answer to all three questions is the same – because exchanges are the best thing to happen to punters in the history of betting.

Think choice, think betting exchanges. Think value, think betting exchanges. Think profits, think betting exchanges.

It's hard to convey just how much impact this relatively new phenomenon has had on the way people bet, but it is at least equal in magnitude to the effects that the arrival of sound and colour had on the film industry or possibly even the invention of the telephone had on communications.

Indeed, it is arguable that had the technology been around in 1961, the year betting shops were legalised, there would have been no need for the dingy smoke-filled parlours that for years were the only outlets for bettors until the internet hit the scene – one of the few things we can thank the US Department of Defence for!

That's because a betting exchange – with Betfair the market leader – is the perfect betting model. It pits punters against punters, both placing bets and taking bets in a marketplace that, for the most part, is so competitive that the prices available beat hands down anything a traditional bookmaker would dare to offer.

So why bet with anyone else?

Many reasons are cited and they range from simple technophobia to concerns about being picked off by shrewd operators and the possibility of corruption.

These are real issues for some people and one of the aims of this book is to allay such fears and, in the case of corruption, do so without the scaremongering that has been a feature of some of the attacks from self-interested parties.

But the main aims are to help punters understand the massive advantages that exchange betting offers, to swerve the costly errors that can easily be avoided with a bit of clear thinking and, most of all, to help to make your exchange punting experience both exciting and profitable.

An attempt has been made to cover most sports, but to do so largely (though not exclusively) from an in-running angle. The reasons for this are twofold.

First, at its most basic level, exchange betting is fixed-odds betting and the type of pre-event analysis needed to get the most out of horse and sports wagering has already been covered in this series of books, of which this is the third.

It would certainly be easy to produce copy by going over old ground, but it wouldn't bring anything new to the table. If you are serious about betting on racing and sport you should read *The Definitive Guide To Betting On Horses* and *The Definitive Guide To Betting On Sport*.

Second, apart from acknowledging that it actually goes on, betting in-running has never been properly covered.

Until the advent of the betting exchanges, once a football match had kicked off, that was the end of betting

It's still a relatively new phenomenon after all, although it has to be acknowledged that in-running punting was around well before exchanges.

The growth in this area of the betting market is largely attributable to go-ahead bookmaker Stan James, one of the first layers to fully recognise its potential. It's amazing when you come to think of it that before the 1990s you could not get a bet on a televised football match after it had started, while we had reached 2000 before bookmakers would even offer you the chance to bet on a non-live football match at half-time.

Now, though, in-running betting has really taken off, with virtually every main-stream bookmaker offering a service on a huge range of sports.

But in-running punting with bookmakers has one massive drawback as by the time you have made a call to your layer the price you were after may have been taken down. And even if it hasn't, the chances are you are betting to stingy percentages as the layers make efforts to cover themselves in such a fast-moving betting medium. That's why exchanges should be the clear choice for in-running punters. It's a case of fastest finger first, with split-second requests met with split-second answers.

And the range of in-running options on an exchange far exceeds anything your bookmaker would dare to offer. For a start, exchanges are the only option for punters who want to bet in-running on horses. And given the amount of race-to-race trade on Betfair every day, there is a big demand for it.

And the ability to lay selections provides a hedging mechanism of a quality that has never been available to fixed-odds punters before, which in turn has brought into being a new type of punter – the trader.

If you are interested only in whether your judgement is right or wrong then trading is probably not for you, but if you want to make money regardless of the end result on the medium you are betting on you will not find any other platform that offers such a golden chance.

And you will soon see that fears of being taken apart by this new breed of super-shrewd gambler are totally unfounded. Betting in-running will provide you with the opportunity to take advantage of some of the weaknesses in human nature. Most punters are losers and always will be, with greed, gullibility and downright stupidity all in evidence every single day on an exchange.

This is a golden age for the serious gambler and no-one should get left behind.

The dinosaurs went extinct, and while betting shop punters may be around for a long while yet, their money, as always, is on the endangered list.

With an exchange, your betting bank might just continue to evolve. ■

learning about the basics

GETTING STARTED

By PAUL KEALY

IF YOU HAVEN'T GOT YOURSELF an account with a betting exchange it really is about time you saw the error of your ways.

If you are in any way interested in obtaining value for money from your punting you should immediately dispel any doubts you have about exchanges, jump on the bandwagon and enjoy the ride to punting nirvana.

The aim of this chapter is to give the novice punter an idea of how an exchange works and explaining how to get started.

WHAT IS AN EXCHANGE?

Despite what traditional high street layers would have you believe, all betting exchanges are in fact licensed bookmakers.

However, they are bookies with a difference because they never take any risk – at least this is true of those exchanges which have a big enough client base not to have to put their own money in.

The nearest model to a betting exchange has been in circulation for nearly 100 years and if you have been to a horse or a greyhound meeting at some stage in your life you will almost certainly have used one. It's called the Tote.

The first automatic totalisator machine was installed at Ellerslie Racecourse in New Zealand in 1913 and was quickly copied around the world. The French call it pari-mutuel, which translated into English means bet-mutual. In other words, it means betting among ourselves.

And for many exchange punters you can translate it even further: it means dispensing with bookmakers altogether. And why should we be so keen to do that?

Bookmakers work to fairly rigid profit margins depending on how many runners there are. Effectively what they are doing is offering prices so that if they lay an even spread of money, they will win whatever happens.

For example, in a three-runner race where all contestants have the same chance of winning, the true odds of each winning are 2-1. A bookmaker would more likely offer 7-4 about each, meaning that if he took £400 at 7-4 on all three contenders, he would lose £700 to whoever backed the winner, but win £400 from each of the two losing bets, giving him a guaranteed profit of £100.

That is how bookmakers have worked for years.

The table (right) is included to give you an idea of how betting percentages work. Whenever studying prices for an event you should work out the percentages from the best prices for each contender. The nearer you get to 100 per cent, the more value there is for the backer. Dip below 100 and it is possible to make money by backing all selections in the same event.

And a betting exchange is a super-competitive market place where the percentages for layers only just creep over the magical figure of 100. Many layers are fighting for your money and with no overheads to talk of they can afford to offer better prices than the high street firms.

The sting in the tail for backers and layers is a commission charge on winnings. On Betfair, by far the largest of the exchanges, commission is charged on a sliding scale of 2-5 per cent depending on your turnover. Very few punters will ever get down below

ODDS AS PERCENTAGES

Odds on	price	odds against
50.00	Evens	50.00
51 22	21-20	48.78
52 38	11-10	47 62
54 55	6-5	45 45
55.56	54	44 44
56 52	13-10	43.48
57 89	11-8	42 11
58.33	7-5	41 87
60.00	B4	40.00
61 54	8-5	38.48
81 90	13-8	38.10
63.64	74	36.36
E4.29	9-5	35.71
65.22	15 8	34.78
86 67	2-1	33.33
66 00	8540	32 00
66 75	11-5	31 25
69 23	94	30 77
70 37	9540	29 63
70 59	12-5	29 41
7143	5-2	28 57
72.22	13-5	27 78
73.33	114	26.67
73.68	14-5	26.32
75.00	3-1	25.00
76.19	16-5	23.81
76 92	100-30	23.08
77.27	17-5	22 73
77.78	7-2	22.22
78 28	18-5	21.74
80.00	4-1	20.W
81.82	9-2	18.18
83 33	5-1	16.67
84.62	11-2	15.38
85.71	8-1	14.29
88.67	13-2	13 33
87 50	7-1	12 50
88.24	15-2	11.78
88.89	81	11.11
89 47	17-2	10.53
90 00	9-1	10 00
90 48	19-2	9 52
90 91	101	9.09
91 67	11-1	8.33
92 31	12-1	7 69
92 88	13-1	7 14
93.33	14-1	6 67
93 75	15-1	6.24
94 12	16-1	5 88
95 24	201	4.76
95 65	22-1	4 35
96 15	25-1	3 85
96.55	28-1	3.45
97.06	33-1	2.94
97.56	40-1	2.44
98.04	501	1.96
98 51	66-1	1 49
99 01	1001	0.91

To calculate the percentage each price is worth, add a point and made into 100 So 3-1 becomes four into 100, equals 25.

EFFECT OF COMMISSION ON BETTING EXCHANGE ODDS

Decimal odds	Decimal odds after 5% commission	
	To lay	To back
1.1	1.095	1.105
1.2	1.190	1.211
1.3	1.285	1.316
1.4	1.380	1.421
1.5	1.475	1.526
1.6	1.570	1.632
1.7	1.665	1.737
1.8	1.760	1.842
1.9	1.855	1.947
2.0	1.950	2.053
2.1	2.045	2.158
2.2	2.140	2.263
2.3	2.235	2.368
2.4	2.330	2.474
2.5	2.425	2.579
2.6	2.520	2.684
2.7	2.615	2.789
2.8	2.710	2.895
2.9	2.805	3.000
3.0	2.900	3.105
3.5	3.375	3.632
4.0	3.850	4.158
4.5	4.325	4.684
5.0	4.800	5.211
5.5	5.275	5.737
6.0	5.750	6.263
6.5	6.225	6.789
7.0	6.700	7.316
7.5	7.175	7.842
8.0	7.650	8.368
8.5	8.125	8.895
9.0	8.600	9.421
9.5	9.075	9.947
10.0	9.550	10.474
15.0	14.300	15.737
20.0	19.050	21.000
25.0	23.800	26.263
30.0	28.550	31.526
35.0	33.300	36.789
40.0	38.050	42.053
45.0	42.800	47.316
50.0	47.550	52.579
60.0	57.050	63.105
70.0	66.550	73.632
80.0	76.050	84.158
90.0	85.550	94.684
100.0	95.050	105.211

three per cent, and most will operate at somewhere between four and five per cent.

Commission is charged only on profits within each market. For example, if you have £20 on two selections at 5-1 in the same race and one of them wins, you pay commission on £80 winnings (£100 from your winner less £20 on the loser), which comes to £4 at five per cent.

The table (left) shows how commission rates at five per cent affect the odds. For instance, if you fancy a horse at evens with the major bookmakers, it would have to be on offer at more than 2.1 on an exchange for it to represent better value.

EXPLODING A FEW MYTHS Other than technophobia, one big reason that certain people are wary of exchanges is that they believe they will be picked off by others who are simply too shrewd.

This is an argument I have come across many times, but one that is deeply flawed.

Who are all these shrewdies anyway?

The truth is that for exchanges to work there have to be losers as well as winners. We can't all put our money into a pool and all take more out and the reality is that 90 per cent of punters will be losers wherever they decided to place their bets. How successful you are depends entirely on you. But providing you adopt the same levels of discipline/indiscipline as in your pre-exchange days this is what you can expect from your experience:

If you are a big loser, you will still lose money, but because you are getting better odds, you will take longer to blow your dough.

If you are a small loser in the long run, you may find yourself edging into profit.

If you are a small winner you will find yourself being even more successful.

If you are a decent winner you can expect to win even more money than is already the case now.

There are no downsides here and the reason is quite simple. You are getting better odds. And all this is before you start to take advantage of the new avenues that have been opened up to punters thanks to the advent of betting exchanges.

The whole point of an exchange is value. Imagine walking into Ladbrokes and seeing 28-1 about a golfer you fancy for the British Open. Then you log on to an exchange and see the same man trading a 39-1.

Do you:
A) back him with Ladbrokes?
B) Back him on the exchange?
C) Find someone else to back because the exchange layer clearly knows something?

There seems to be an astonishing number of people that believe the answer is C. To a lot of us, this is too silly for words, but betting is full of conspiracy theorists who see corruption around every corner. You would be amazed at how many people turn down great value bets on the grounds that the price was too big to be true.

Of course, there will always be occasions when some punters (and bookmakers) know more than you and we will deal with those concerns elsewhere later, but more often than not you will be betting against people who simply do not share your views. And when you take the punter-friendly margins into account, you are obviously going to get some very generous odds.

GETTING STARTED
Technophobes beware. One thing you will need to become an exchange punter is a computer. Yes, some exchanges do allow you to bet by telephone, but you will never see the full merits of exchange punting until you are faced by a screen with all the odds in front of you.

First of all, you must register with your chosen exchange and deposit some money. Doing this is remarkably easy. It is simply

---

how the Tote work

 No price control

What happens with a Tote pool is that all punters make their selections and hand over their cash to a third party – the Tote. They are then paid a dividend if they win. This payout depends on how many other people made the same winning selection and, of course, the Tote's takeout, which can be up to 40 per cent of the total pool depending on where you go.

The premise is roughly the same with betting exchanges – you place your money with a third party in order to have it matched against other punters. In this instance, though, you place your money with a request for a price, and if that price is not acceptable with other punters, you will not have a bet.

It gives you the advantage of price control, which is something you never had before with a Tote. You also dispense with the need for a traditional high street layer, which in turns mean you get better value – much better value.

If an exchange offers 39-1 about 25-1 shot like Jim Furyk, just take it

a case of filling in a form on a screen putting in the relevant details where prompted. Once that is done, you are ready to go.

The first time you are confronted by an exchange screen showing odds can be daunting because you are faced with six sets of prices per contender rather than one. But once you get your head round the layout, it is quite simple.

For our beginner's example we'll use a random horse race on Betfair. On the left-hand side of the screen you will be confronted by all the names of the runners (see example page 19).

Next to each runner will be six columns of prices, with the money available to back or lay. The three boxes closest to the selection represent the odds and money available to the backer. The right-hand side of these three – shown in blue – are the best odds at the current time. If you believe this price is acceptable, you simply click on the box and key in your desired stake where prompted and then submit. You will next be asked to confirm that the details are correct and once you have done that your bet will be entered into the system.

This sounds like a lot of button-pressing but in reality it takes only seconds and there is a good reason for exchange sites asking you to confirm your bet before pushing it through – it helps to root out some of the mistakes made by punters clicking the wrong button; laying instead of backing etc.

The next three boxes show the prices available to the layer, but this time the one on the left – usually in pink but you can choose to put the lay side in yellow – represents the best odds available to lay. Again, if the price available to lay is acceptable, you click on that box, enter the size of the bet you wish to take, submit and then confirm. And that is really all there is to placing a bet if you are willing to take the available odds.

However, the beauty of exchanges is that you don't have to accept what is on offer, which is why the other boxes are on show.

For instance, let's say your selection was available to back at 4 (this is 3-1; all exchange odds are displayed in decimals, which are inclusive of stake) and to lay at 5. There is quite a big difference here, and though you might think 4 is a bit stingy, the chance of you getting 5 may also be remote. You can ask for something in between.

Whenever you click on the back/lay boxes you are given the option to accept the current price or request another price. So in this instance you may ask for 4.5. You follow the same routine as before, but this time your wager has been placed as an order on the system and you must wait for someone to accept. Presuming no-one has asked for shorter than 4.5 in the meantime, your request will kick the 5 out of the way on the lay side and will take its place as first in line for potential layers to take.

This takes a bit of monitoring as for some there is nothing more annoying than asking for a price about a winner and then not getting it matched. Others will be perfectly

Current market percentage for backers.

Current market percentage for layers.

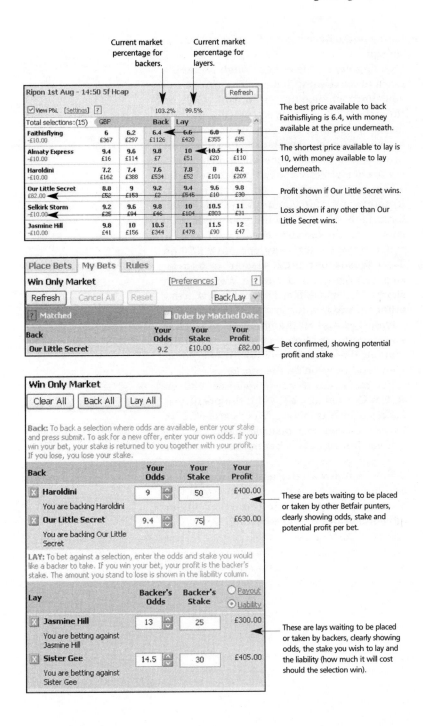

The best price available to back Faithisfliying is 6.4, with money available at the price underneath.

The shortest price available to lay is 10, with money available to lay underneath.

Profit shown if Our Little Secret wins.

Loss shown if any other than Our Little Secret wins.

Bet confirmed, showing potential profit and stake

These are bets waiting to be placed or taken by other Betfair punters, clearly showing odds, stake and potential profit per bet.

These are lays waiting to be placed or taken by backers, clearly showing odds, the stake you wish to lay and the liability (how much it will cost should the selection win).

happy not to have a bet if the price is wrong, though.

In any case, it is easy enough to keep a track of what's happening. The prices will constantly change in front of you, while on the right of the screen you can click on "My Bets" which will tell you all you need to know. You can also choose to view your profit/loss figures for each selection by clicking the box directly above the top contender which says view P&L. On Betfair this is usually set up for you anyway. When you have done this, the amount you win/lose on each runner is shown below its name.

For instance, let's say you have £50 on Tiger Woods for the US Masters at 6 (5-1). In green figures underneath Woods it will show £250, while in red figures below every other runner it will show -£50 because you obviously lose £50 if anybody else wins. If you have more than one bet on the same market, these figures will take into account your total position on the market.

For instance, if you also have £30 on Retief Goosen at 12 (11-1), the profit/loss figures will be as follows: Woods green £220, Goosen green £280, rest red -£80.

If you haven't had a bet matched, nothing will appear.

That is really all there is to placing a bet, and once you have got used to it you will soon come to discover the other major advantages of exchange betting. ■

andrew black realises a dream

HOW IT ALL STARTED

By PAUL KEALY

**Betfair founder
Andrew Black**

ANDREW BLACK HAS, AMONG other things, variously been described as scruffy, eccentric, a former professional poker and bridge player, golf caddie and inventor of the betting exchange.

He is all of those except one.

And, surprisingly enough, it's the one he gets all the credit for. So let's say it loud and clear: Black is not responsible for the idea of the betting exchange – but he is the man who made it work.

When I asked him which exchange was first on the scene, Betfair or Flutter.com, the answer came as quite a surprise. "Neither," he said. "BetEx has been around for eight years. That was mostly really a fax service, though."

So the idea of matching bets between punters directly and therefore kicking out the middle man's risk (margin) has been around for quite some time and Black, though justifiably proud of his achievements, is neither arrogant nor big-headed. If he is going to be given any credit, he would like to be recognised for his 'big ideas' and not those of others.

In a time when the phrase is ludicrously overused, the 42-year-old truly is one of life's original thinkers and according to him he has had "three really big ideas to do with exchanges. And only two of them worked."

This is the story of how Black's Betfair became the betting exchange behemoth, while others withered and died, were swallowed up, or now simply scrabble around for a few crumbs.

Black claims that an urge to gamble has been in the family for generations, which would not normally be a surprising statement were it not for the fact that his grandfather, former Conservative MP Sir Cyril Black, was a deeply religious anti-gambling campaigner.

"It's the usual story really," he says. "My grandmother on my mother's side always liked a bet; my first bet on a horse was a winner, that sort of thing."

Indeed, gambling began to take up so much of Black's time that he soon found himself in trouble, not with his finances as he had already developed the knack of winning, but with education, and he wound up being kicked out of Exeter University for failing in his first year.

It wasn't until he was 26 that Black actually got a 'proper' job, working for a US derivatives company, but even then he was never far away from the punting scene. Jobs were always failing to provide a sufficient challenge or he would fall out with his employers, so in the end he went it alone, but moved away from the City trading scene and towards the internet, which was becoming seriously big business.

"I started looking for internet work," he said. "You could say I was fairly webby. I was very impressed with the success of the likes of Yahoo and eBay."

By the late 1990s all the bits and pieces of Black's big idea were falling into place. He knew gambling, he knew the internet and he knew all about the stock exchange.

"Suddenly it all came to me," he said. "I realised how it should all work. Think of

uncommon knowledge

 the almost invincible system

Gambling was a way of life for Andrew Black from an early age and if he hadn't made a fortune out of Betfair, he probably would be taking bookies to the cleaners to this day. Working for others just never seemed to be his thing. "I knew gambling inside out," says Black without a trace of conceit. It's just a fact. "I had been betting in bookies since I was 18, playing poker, and I had written all sorts of odds-analysis and programs and they always made money."

One he could never quite get to grips with – still can't, in fact – was his football betting programme, which produced a system that was "unbeatable" but only until Christmas.

"I could make a fortune out of betting on football with this system from September to December," he says. "It was invincible. It once produced a price of 6-4 for a 0-0 draw between Leeds and Aston Villa. It had not come up with anything lower than 3-1 for that scoreline before, but sure enough, the game was goalless. But after Christmas the system was completely hopeless. I never managed to work out why. One day I hope to sit down and have another go at it."

the New York Stock Exchange. You have a commodity listed with people putting up bids and taken them down again. On show are the price and the number of units available at the price.

"You could easily transfer that to betting – you have the odds on show and the money available at which to bet. This was the big idea. I dreamed about it all night and I was more afraid of not following it through than going for it."

Regular users of exchanges, whether on Betfair or any of the much smaller ones around today, could be forgiven for thinking 'so what?'

Familiarity with the model – now used by all exchanges – blinds us to the originality of the concept and it is hard to think of another way in which an exchange could be presented.

We shall soon see otherwise, but that's jumping the gun just a little. Black now needed to get some money on board to develop his new idea, and with the dot.com boom about to implode, it was not easy.

He teamed up with Edward Wray, the brother of his best friend Jeremy.

Black and Wray are co-founders of Betfair, and Black is keen to acknowledge that without Wray's business knowledge the venture may never have got off the ground. "He really gets things done," said Black.

But the one thing they couldn't do was find anyone in the City to invest in their idea and despite raising £1m from family and friends they were at a massive financial disadvantage for the battle that was to come.

As mentioned earlier, the betting exchange concept was not the brainchild of Black, and there were several other exchanges being primed to hit the market, more or less at the same time.

And to a certain extent it was a race against time as very early in the development of his idea, Black had come to the conclusion that the winner would soon have virtual dominance over the exchange scene.

"It's a rare case of being a natural monopoly," he says. "That's because we provide the marketplace for punters to compete."

And you can't have a marketplace of marketplaces.

Having put together a team of some "seriously brilliant people", Betfair suffered a blow when flutter.com launched in April 2000, nearly two months before Betfair was ready to go.

But though privately admitting to sleepless nights as the Betfair model was going through the design stage, Black says he was always quietly confident that none of his rivals would have the complete package.

"My idea had taken two years to develop and some of these firms were rushing theirs out within a couple of months," he says. "Without being cocky, I was sure they couldn't possibly produce what we were about to deliver."

uncommon
knowledge

 rivals steal a march

Flutter was just one of three firms (the others were Betmart and Betswap) preparing to hit the market. It was headed by Josh Hannah who, with an MBA from Stanford University and a BA from the University of California in Berkeley, had skipped across the pond to develop his idea of person-to-person betting because a website allowing people to bet among themselves would have been illegal in the States.

And unlike Black and Wray, the former venture capitalist with Bain and Co brought some serious backing. Hannah had secured some $43.7m, which gave him a big head-start, especially in terms of marketing.

Within two months of their launch in April 2000, Flutter had become commercial partners for Channel 4's Big Brother and had signed a partnership deal with travel website lastminute.com.

They were fastest out of the blocks and were getting plenty of exposure.

And though not everyone at Betfair shared his unshakeable faith, Black claims Flutter's launch served only to confirm that his was the winning formula.

"They got it badly wrong," he says dismissively, although the look in his eyes betrayed the fact that early competition was quite bitter. "We wanted to kill them and they wanted to kill us," he admits.

Ask Black where Flutter made their mistakes and you soon run out of notepaper. We'll cut it down to the major ones.

"They based themselves on eBay and targeted the mass market," explained Black. "Everything was displayed as if on a billboard, and bets were like 'Who is going to be on page 3 tomorrow?' They assumed there was an enormous market for such simple things.

"There was no racing to start with and no Rule 4. It was a shark pool."

Placing multiple bets on the same market – in particular lays – required vast sums on money way in excess of the true liability.

"They didn't seem to understand that more than one lay in the same market actually reduced the liability," added Black. This meant that if you wanted to lay £100 of four selections in the same event, say at 2-1, 3-1, 4-1 and 5-1, you had to stump up the liability for each bet.

So while Betfair would hold just £200 of your money (the worst case scenario was if the 5-1 shot won, losing you £500 although you recouped £300 by laying three losers), Flutter would take £1,400. It didn't add up.

Placing bets was also a complete nightmare, as Black explained. "There was no structure at all. If you wanted £100 at 2-1, your bet had to be taken in its entirety by one person. They couldn't offer to lay £20 of it and leave the rest for someone else. If you wanted to get a decent bet on you would have to put up 20 bets of £5 or ten of £10. It was very time-consuming,

uncommon knowledge

 why decimals work best

Derek McGovern wrote in the *Daily Mirror* that Betfair would never catch on in Britain because of their use of decimal odds.

This is what McGovern said: "I've always predicted that betting exchanges will fail to hook Britain's punting public because of one big failing ... their suicidal policy of using decimal, rather than fractional, odds.

"Punters in Britain have been brought up on 11-10, on 9-4, on 100-30. It's a language we've all become fluent in. It's our mother tongue. But the betting exchanges have demanded we learn another tongue. In their world 11-10 is not 11-10, it's 2.10; 9-4 is 3.25; and even the simple 10-1 is 11.00.

"Why? What in God's name was wrong with the fractions? I understood that Andre Agassi was hot favourite to win in Rome yesterday when I saw odds of 2-7. But his decimal odds of 1.29 meant nothing."

But apart from being wrong with his prediction because Betfair is already arguably the biggest betting website in the world with a huge British client base, McGovern's argument betrays a complete failure to understand the dynamics of exchange betting.

According to Andrew Black, decimal odds had to be the way forward, and were one of the reasons (though there were many) that punters chose his model over Flutter and the others.

Traditional, much-loved shows of 6-4, 9-4 and 7-2 are perfectly convenient for bookmakers, who work with nice big profit margins but they don't operate as anywhere near as effectively on an exchange, where competition forces the margin down to less than one per cent in many cases.

The problem for those who like traditional odds is that the difference between prices on the usual scale is too big. For instance, the recognised next step up from 6-4 (2.5 in decimals) is 13-8. On Betfair you can get six price increments (2.52, 2.54, 2.56, 2.58, 2.6 and 2.62) before the next one carries you past 13-8.

So when you apply the traditional style of displaying odds on an exchange, the system soon breaks down and instead of looking at nice, easily-recognisable numbers that British punters have grown up with, you are faced with something far more confusing than decimals ever could be.

And that's what happened on Flutter, according to Black: "If you wanted to lay something for £100 at evens, someone would leapfrog you and go 100/99," he said. "Then someone else would go 99/98, and someone else 98/97. The difference in price was tiny and the odds unworkable. What was needed was a structure where price increments are large enough to make a difference, sufficiently small to allow competition and immediately understandable. Our decimal pricing system is perfect."

So when discussing the merits of traditional odds over decimals, McGovern should ask himself which of the following bets is easiest to work out: £100 at 2.02 or £100 at 97/95; £100 at 1.39 or £100 at 37/94?

not to mention irritating. On Betfair if you put up a bet of £50 it's quite likely that it is being taken by more than one person."

Black was convinced he had got it right, and was more confident than ever that his firm would run out comfortable winners after Betmart and Betswap adopted the Flutter model. But he still needed to get word out about his website, had very little money to pay for advertising and limited outlets in which to push his business.

"The *Racing Post* thought we were some fly-by-night firm that wouldn't last five minutes so they wouldn't take our money," he said. "I suppose I can see their point now, but it hardly helped at the time."

In the end Betfair had to resort to gimmicks. They included hiring the Sports Café in London's Haymarket for a promotional day and staging a mock funeral march for the 'Death of the Bookmaker' through the streets of London.

The idea was to have an open coffin, with a bookmaker lying in state replete with filthy anorak, cigar and other stereotypical bookie accessories, with people handing out flyers saying something like 'Ban Betfair, it will kill the bookmaking industry.'

An agency for out-of-work actors had provided the bodies and everything was in place until, amazingly, someone else did exactly the same thing and was roundly slated in the press.

"They were funeral firm, of all things," said Black. "Imagine a funeral firm making fun of the funeral business in such a way. Our idea worked – and it was fun."

It also generated just enough publicity – including a photo shoot in *The Times* – to set the ball rolling and the company went live for the first time on 9 June 2000, with the Vodafone Oaks their very first market.

They matched bets totalling £3,462 – a drop in the ocean, but they were under way.

And once punters made their first visit they tended to stay. Within ten months Betfair was boasting (on the home page of their website) of £1m in matched bets per week, after another eight months it was £10m and by 2003 was £50m. They boast no more, however.

Edward Wray (left) and Andrew Black pose with 'dead' bookmaker

"It was important for a while for people to see we were a vibrant company, who could match demand," says Black. "But it was a meaningless number, if truth be told, and after a while people interpreted it as actually meaning something."

Business really took off after the implementation of the third of his big ideas, No. 2 having proved a disappointing failure.

This was in-running betting. "There was obviously a market for it, but I really wanted to make it fair," explained Black.

"I didn't want it to turn into some fastest-finger joke. It's still a bit about the fastest reaction but there had to be some protection both for backers and layers – some way of changing your mind and getting out of the situation if the need arises."

So Black devised a time-delay system, which he still believes is misunderstood. On most sports there is a five-second time delay on placing bets. Once you hit that button, it takes five seconds for your request to appear on the site. Yet if it is not matched and something has happened that

uncommon
knowledge

 **fluffing
his lines**

Black still has a look of
surprise on his face at
the failure of his second
big idea – line betting.
In America, the
under/over market for
points on American
football is very popular,
with punters being
asked to bet high or
low. It's really a fixed-
odds spread bet.

"The idea is that the
odds always remain
evens," says Black.

"But the line moves
up or down depending
on demand. I was sure
it was going to be a
winner but it didn't
work at all."
Betfair still offers some
line bets, like winning
distances on horse
racing, but not many.
"I still think it should be
more popular than it
is," added Black.

makes you alter your view about the bet
you can cancel it immediately.

"We still get people asking us to get rid
of the time delay altogether, but we would
be wrong to do so. It is fair and it works."

Everything suddenly appeared too much
for Flutter, and though rumours were sug-
gesting they were eating into Betfair's
market dominance by the end of 2001,
they had also spent virtually every penny
of their investor's money.

And so, in January 2002, Betfair made
their move and took over Flutter, thus
claiming a massive 98 per cent of the
market.

With the emergence of the likes of
Betdaq, the figure nomally bandied around
nowdays is 90 per cent, but whatever the
case, they are the true giant of exchange
betting.

It is an open secret that one day Betfair
will be floated on the Stock Exchange,
making Black an extremely rich man. In
2005 he appeared on the Times Rich List
with an estimated wealth of £75m, but
other estimates reckon a float could see
him being worth more than twice that.

But whatever happens, Black won't rest
on his laurels. Like most entrepreneurs he
is too much of a thinker to be spending the
rest of his life with his feet up on a fantasy
island.

Who knows? He might just have another
big idea.

"Big? I doubt it. But I've got a few
smaller ones that I'd like to pursue."

Someone had better watch out. ■

a hatful of advantages

CHANGING THE WAY WE BET

THERE IS LITTLE DOUBT THAT By PAUL KEALY
exchanges are changing the shape of betting, not just in this country but worldwide. More and more punters are realising that you don't have to run with a position from start to finish and that you can trade your way to profit without taking a risk.

Such options are simply not available with the high street bookies, whose margins allow little room for manoeuvring. It cannot be stated often enough that one of the big advantages exchanges offer is terrific value prices, but that is only half the story.

Outlined in these pages are the ways in which betting exchanges have improved the life of the punter.

LAYING The ability to lay a selection to lose has caused uproar among bookies but, as usual, they are barking up the wrong tree. We will come to that argument later in the book, but for now we will concentrate on what great news it is for us.

One of the most obvious advantages in laying comes from the ability to oppose a poor-value favourite without having to place several bets to do so. Now you can simply lay away to your heart's content.

For instance, you think a 5-4 favourite will not perform well on the soft ground. In the past, in order to oppose it you would have to back every other runner, working out how much to have on each in order to return the same winnings if the hotpot loses. And without exchanges you would be getting incredibly bad value because you would have to take into account the bookmakers' profit margins.

Here's an example: in an all-weather flat race in March 2005, the favourite finished with an SP of 5-4. The rest of the field were priced at: 3-1, 9-1, 9-1, 10-1, 14-1, 20-1 and 33-1. Using the table on page 14 we can work out that the combined percentage about all the runners other than the favourite is roughly 68.5. That is somewhere between 1-2 and 4-9. So to oppose a 5-4 shot and be certain to win if it got beat, you would have to bet at around 4-9. And this is an example taken from when the existence of betting exchanges had already resulted in what the bookies have called an adverse effect on their profit margins. In other words, without exchanges that 4-9 would almost certainly be even shorter.

But that is all in the past. Now, at the click of a button you can replace all the hard work with a simple lay of the jolly. Beware, though, you will almost certainly not be able to lay it at 5-4. Betting exchanges, remember, offer terrific value to the punter. To be a full-time layer you are forced to work to tiny percentages. Still, the chances are you will be happily accommodated at 6-4 (which is 4-6 to you) and that's a damn sight better than you could expect from your local bookie.

HEDGING gives you the opportunity to ensure that whatever happens in a given sporting event, you cannot lose.

Obviously, you have to get yourself into a position whereby your original bet has shortened or your lay has drifted. Let's say that you have had £20 on a golfer at 50-1 and he stands two shots clear going into the final round. He may be on offer at 2.5 on Betfair, in which case there are several options open to you.

You could simply lay £20 at 2.5, thereby ensuring you don't lose anything, or you could lay a much bigger chunk, say £400, thus ensuring that you win £380 if he loses and £400 if he wins.

Again, such an option without betting exchanges is virtually non-existent. Your bookmaker might be offering 11-10 about your selection, but to cover your money you would have to back all the other possible winners and, with players like Padraig Harrington, who came back from seven strokes behind to win the Honda Classic in March 2005, you are never going to beat the profit margin.

The argument over whether it is a correct strategy to hedge has been raging for years. There are two basic arguments, and both seem pretty sound.

CASE AGAINST: Every bet should be judged on its merits. It's wrong to take a profit unless you are sure the second bet is a good one. If you think your selection now truly represents an even money chance, you should be having more on at 2.5, not laying it back.

CASE FOR: Everyone knows how hard it is to back winners. We have all at one stage suffered an untimely hit by a last-fence fall, last-minute goal, outrageous chip-in from a bunker, etc. What you are faced with when you are in a good hedging position is effectively free money. Take it, because if you can ensure yourself a no-lose book, you will win money in the long run.

Padraig Harrington was a non-exchange hedger's nightmare when winning the 2005 Honda Classic from seven shots back

Again, it all depends on your point of view, but after years of being an out and out punter I am finally coming round to the idea of hedging.

And here's just one reason why. A colleague of mine at the *Racing Post* stood to win £9,000 on Henrik Stenson in the Qatar Masters in 2005. Stenson traded at 1.6 during the final round on Betfair but got beaten. My colleague, not having a hedging mentality, blew the chance to guarantee himself up to five grand.

Obviously it works the other way round as well. You can hedge, see your original bet win and feel sick as a parrot at having given so much money away.

However, the majority of us back many more losers than winners, and I have a gut feeling that most punters would be better off if they regularly took insurance.

TRADING Mention the word "trader" to anyone and they instinctively think of someone who works the stock market

uncommon knowledge

 a hedge can be bad value

There is one problem with hedging on the likes of Betfair and it's one that all punters have to come to grips with.

As the argument goes, the case against hedging is that you should only hedge if the second bet is a good one.

Unfortunately, if you are laying on Betfair, you are, almost without exception, offering excellent value to the backer.

And this is especially true of markets like golf tournaments. Here's an example: in the 2003 US PGA Championship, I backed Justin Leonard at average odds of 65.

Going into the final round, Leonard was three shots clear of Rich Beem and four ahead of Fred Funk, with five strokes back to Tiger Woods. Not surprisingly, he was a very short price with the high street firms – as low as 2-7.

However, on Betfair layers were giving Leonard away at 1.63 – that's around 8-13. I could not bring myself to lay him back at that price, and so ended up with nothing after his final-round 77.

The problem is that this is not a one-off. Many people like to hedge nowadays, and the market is so competitive that they are falling over themselves to lay a price.

The question is: do you place a bad value bet to cover yourself? It's a tricky one.

buying and selling shares. Buy low, sell high, and you can't lose.

Now, thanks to the exchange revolution, which allows you to back and lay, you can trade horses, dogs, golfers, anything you can bet on – and stacks of punters are taking advantage of this new avenue.

Everything is a commodity on an exchange market and if you call it right you can make money even before an event has started.

A trader's unique skill is not knowing what a price should be, but what it will be. He could not care less about finding the winner.

An insight into how other people will bet (how the market will react) is a licence to print money on Betfair whether you identify an upcoming gamble or a drifter in the betting. The strategy behind it is simple enough, although it takes a fair degree of skill.

Let's say you have identified a 6-1 shot, which you are pretty sure will shorten throughout the day and may start at around 3-1.

You place £200 at 6-1, wait for it to shorten and then lay it back. You could lay £200 at 3-1 and give yourself a free £600 bet, or simply lay £350 at 3-1 and show no more interest in the event safe in the knowledge that you have made £150 whatever happens.

Obviously that is a rather simple example and in practice it is rarely that easy, but there are many traders who make a comfortable living by never taking a position and they can do so even if the difference in price is only a few hundredths of a point. All you need is plenty of money in your account to do so and the ability to call it right.

Indeed, it could be argued that while Betfair can boast some 350,000 users (70,000 active in any week) they are powered by a small percentage – the traders, who offer prices on both sides (back and lay) and take what small commission they can in between.

Just like the stock market, the Betfair market is constantly fluctuating, meaning traders can dip in an out when it suits them – often using hi-tech computer programmes to help them do so. They provide the liquidity on which Betfair thrives, while making their own, no-risk profit.

Securing a no-lose book on one runner or covering all eventualities for guaranteed profit is generally referred to as arbitrage.

In finance theory, an arbitrage is defined as a transaction or portfolio that makes a profit without risk. More formally, a portfolio is said to be an arbitrage if it costs nothing to implement, has a positive probability of a positive payoff, and a zero probability of a negative payoff.

BETTING IN-RUNNING Imagine backing a horse in a six-furlong sprint at 16-1 and watching it blast from the stalls and into a three-length lead after a furlong. It still holds that lead entering the last furlong, but confidence in your bet being a winner is low because you are pretty sure the jockey has set off too fast.

Sure enough, with 100 yards to run the beast is treading water, the jockey getting more and more urgent and the pack closing in fast. You get nailed long before the line.

Sound familiar? So it should, as this sort of scenario unfolds virtually every day on the racecourse and there are similar hard-luck stories in every sport you can bet on.

And until the advent of exchanges there was nothing you could do about it except take on the chin and hope your luck improved next time. It's a different ball game now, though.

You can offer/ask for a price even in the last ten yards of a race

Betting in-running is not a new phenome-non – Stan James is one bookmaking firm which has led the way – but in-running betting on horseracing is the sole domain of betting exchanges. Indeed, having looked at all the major firms, it's fair to say that if you want to bet in-running on horses and pretty much every sport, Betfair is the place to go.

In-running betting is where many traders make their killing, taking advantage of the rapid fluctuations in the market. Much of this book is devoted to in-running action, so there is little need to delve too deeply here.

PLACE BACKING/LAYING Straight-forward win betting is hardly revolutionary, but place-only betting is virtually unique to exchanges. The exceptions are, of course, the Tote, where you have to put up with extortionate deductions from the pool, and golf.

Some bookmakers now offer top-five finish markets in all golf tournaments, and thankful though we are, the layers are not taking too much of a risk when the average field size is 156 runners.

But on the exchanges you can bet place only on any event in which the bookies offer each-way betting.

uncommon knowledge

playing with percentages

At the *Racing Post* we often receive calls from punters asking how to work out betting percentages. While there is a table on page 14 that shows percentages, it is actually quite an easy process. You simply add a point to the price and divide it into 100. Therefore, 2-1 becomes 100/3=33.33. In the case of decimal prices, which include the stake and which you will see on the exchanges, you simply devide the price into 100. Therefore 3.5 (5-2 in traditional fractions) is simply 100/3.5=28.57 per cent.

Percentages are also the perfect guide for novice arbitrageurs. Let's say you have uncovered a three-runner market in which you can cover the field and make a profit. You need to know exactly how much to have on each to return the same amount. And percentages tell you this.

Keeping it simple, we'll say for argument's sake that the three eventualities are quoted in various places at top prices of evens (50 per cent), 3-1 (25 per cent) and 4-1 (20 per cent), giving a 95 per cent book. For every £100 you wish to return, you have £50 at evens, £25 at 3-1 and £20 at 4-1. Your total stake is £95 and your total return is £100 whatever the result.

This is a major advantage for punters, although you should not fall into the trap of thinking that the odds you will get will correspond exactly to a horse's win chance and in some cases an each-way bet with the bookies will still offer the best value even if the win part is being thrown away.

For example, in an eight-runner race with two stand-out contenders, the prices might be something like 1-2, 9-4, 14-1, 33-1, 33-1, 50-1, 66-1 and 66-1.

The place part of an each-way bet on the 14-1 chance pays 14-5, but you won't get near that on an exchange. In fact, you will probably be offered odds-on.

In circumstances like this it is almost always better to have an each-way bet with a bookie even if you consider your win chances to be virtually non-existent. But in several cases place-only betting on an exchange will offer you tremendous value. Outsiders can often be available to back for a place at up to half their betting shop win price – and sometimes even bigger than their betting shop win price.

I'm Spartacus winning at York on 13 May 2005

Place betting is not something that interests everyone, but the liquidity in Betfair's place markets is growing all the time and there is one sure sign that such an option is excellent for punters – bookmakers won't let you do it.

Place laying can also prove extremely profitable, especially if you are willing to swim against the tide and ignore the talking horses.

There is a superb example of this from the Dante meeting at York in 2005, when the Sir Michael Stoute-trained Blue Train was backed off the boards for, coincindentally, the betfair.com Handicap over an extended ten furlongs.

This was a six-runner race, but eight had been declared and Betfair's place betting terms do not change when there are non-runners so there were still three places up for grabs.

Blue Train had previously won a bog-standard all-weather maiden at Wolverhampton in a slow time, sufficiently slow to return a *Racing Post* Topspeed figure lower than any of his opponents, one of which was Dee Stakes second I'm Spartacus, who was officially 21lb well-in according to the handicapper.

But none of this seemed to matter with punters, who forced Blue Train down to 6-5 favouritism and 1-10 in the place market. Rumours were apparently rife on the racecourse that this was Stoute's Derby horse. Why Stoute wasn't running it in the Dante (won by his Derby winners North Light and Sharastani), Dee Stakes (Shergar and Kris Kin), or Sandown Classic Trial (Shergar again) didn't seem to matter.

This was a typical example of a talking horse and 1.1 layers cleaned up when Blue Train trailed in last. ■

why betfair stands alone

THE MAJOR PLAYERS

THERE'S EASY MONEY TO MADE   By PAUL KEALY
running a betting exchange, isn't there?
Just provide the platform, let the punters
get on with it and take the commission
when it rolls in.

Er, no.

It's amazing how many people seem to
think that running a betting exchange is a
licence to print money, but nothing could
be further from the truth, especially when
Betfair have such a major share of the
market.

Monopolies are often not a good thing,
which is why the Monopolies Commission
exists, but the dynamics of exchange
betting make it very difficult for more than
a couple of firms to be truly competitive –
and earn a crust at the same time. And
some people would argue that there is
room for only one.

That hasn't stopped many investors from
having a crack, though, and in November
2004 there were, amazingly, just under 40
betting exchanges fighting for your hard-
earned.

By the middle of 2005 several of those

had gone to the wall, with the most high-profile, Sporting Options, hitting the skids early in 2005.

There are still several exchanges on the market, but many of these are unlikely to be around for long, so choosing who to open an account with is not necessarily about where the best value lies or what special offers are on the table. Some may tempt you with promises of low commission rates or even no commission, but you would be right to be wary of such offers.

So who is the best firm to bet with, and is it worth opening accounts with everyone?

I thought the best way to address these questions was via an experiment, picking out a high-profile sporting event and comparing prices, market moves and liquidity at various times on various exchanges.

If you go to bettingmarket.com, you can find a list with links to almost 40 betting exchanges.

I am not going to bother listing them all here, however, as most are a complete waste of time to look at. They carry next to no liquidity (meaning there is very little money available at which to back or lay most selections) or bet to percentages that offer no advantage to the backer or layer, which usually means they are seeded. Links to others reveal them to be 'temporarily down for maintenance' (code for 'defunct for good'), while others (Betmate.com, abex88.com) turned out to be Betdaq in disguise.

I have chosen to compare seven exchanges. Two of them, Betfair and Betdaq, will be well known to most punters, while the others are a little more obscure, although some carry enough liquidity to at least be worth another glance.

There are few bigger betting events during a football season than a Champions League semi-final second leg between Liverpool and Chelsea, especially with the tie all-square after the opening encounter at Stamford

Many exchanges had packed up betting even before Liverpool had scored against Chelsea in the 2005 Champions League semi-final

Bridge, so that 2005 contest appeared the ideal medium for our experiment.

The accompanying table on page 44 shows the betting for the Anfield match on the day at midday, 7.30pm – 15 minutes before kick-off – and 8.15 when Liverpool had taken the lead. Under each price is the amount of money available to back or lay at the price. The final line shows the total percentage in each firm's back and lay markets. The lower the percentage on the back side, the more value there is for backers, while the higher the percentage on the lay side, the more value there is for layers.

Taking the midday market first, you will notice that Betfair and Betdaq have a virtual monopoly on the best prices. The best place to back or lay Chelsea or Liverpool is with either Betdaq or Betfair, while only Betbull, Betonbet and Parbet can match the other two on the back price for the draw.

There is also quite clearly far more money available on Betdaq and Betfair – the £10 at 2.27 to lay on Betdaq for

Chelsea was backed up by a huge chunk at 2.28 just behind – than anywhere else.

In the second box, the two main firms again have a virtual monopoly on the best value.

Things change quite dramatically at 8.15pm, by which time Liverpool have a 1-0 lead.

First of all, Back And Lay, Parbet and Redbet have suspended betting. They do not offer an in-running service. This is bad news for anyone who wants to trade out of a position.

Let's say you've had £100 on Liverpool at Parbet's 3.7 (thus already taking the joint-worst exchange price available) and now want to get your stake back. You have to go to a different firm to do so.

It is the same with Redbet and Back And Lay. Trading and the ability to manage your position in any market is one of the main advantages of exchange betting and those not offering such a service would not get any of my money.

They may do so in the future, so are worth watching out for, but the fact remains their prices are very rarely competitive with other exchanges. With their low margins, they will always outdo any given bookmaker, but would probably struggle to offer great value against the whole field.

Those three eliminated, we are now down to four, although it could be argued we are down to two already, given the tendency for Betdaq and Betfair to provide the best prices. And, as far as I am concerned, the other two go on to disqualify themselves anyway.

For a start, neither offers English or Irish horseracing. You can bet on trotting from Gelsenkirchen with Betbull if that is your thing and various other trotting venues with both firms are available but British racing is excluded.

Of course, racing may not be your bag anyway, but we have already seen by the

EXCHANGE BETTING COMPARISON FOR 2005 CHAMPIONS LEAGUE SEMI-FINAL SECOND LEG

Midday	*Back And Lay*		*Betbull*		*Betfair*	
Liverpool	3.8	4	3.7	4.1	3.85	3.9
	£106	£10	£1,229	£984	£6,093	£7,580
Chelsea	2.2	2.35	2.2	2.36	2.28	2.3
	£184	£175	£2,366	£1,918	£46,619	£29,643
Draw	3.2	3.4	3.25	3.4	3.25	3.3
	£10	£122	£139	£984	£53,151	£41,447
Total percentage	103	96.9	103	96	100.6	99.4

7.30	*Back And Lay*		*Betbull*		*Betfair*	
Liverpool	3.85	4	3.65	3.95	3.85	3.9
	£10	£101	£1,254	£715	£16,682	£33,962
Chelsea	2.25	2.375	2.26	2.34	2.34	2.36
	£184	£175	£1,569	£4	£8,971	£64,564
Draw	3.15	3.25	3.18	3.35	3.15	3.2
	£107	£10	£537	£1,265	£13,535	£17,636
Total percentage	102	98	103	97.4	100.4	99.2

8.15pm (1-0)	*Back And Lay*		*Betbull*		*Betfair*	
Liverpool	—	—	1.9	2	1.92	1.93
	—	—	£505	£1,000	£3,916	£3,019
Chelsea	—	—	4.5	5	4.6	4.7
	—	—	£356	£142	£255	£313
Draw	—	—	3.5	3.5	3.65	3.75
	—	—	£400	£192	£2,234	£222
Total percentage	—	—	103.4	93.6	101.2	99.8

betting margins offered by both firms, they are unlikely to be your best option very often. Indeed, the fact that there is often a difference of five per cent in the margin between their back and lay prices suggests at least an element of seeding. Again, this is no bad thing as long as you can guarantee that your money is safe.

And, for the reasons outlined earlier – almost half the betting exchanges in circulation in 2004 were not around in 2005 –

Betdaq		Betonbet		Parbet		Redbet	
3.9	4	3.75	3.95	3.7	3.95	3.76	4.09
£162	£889	£1,077	£49	£979	£30	£1,022	£1,054
2.26	2.27	2.2	2.3	2.22	2.43	2.21	2.34
£20,114	£10	£2,767	£411	£45	£324	£6,387	£6,590
3.25	3.3	3.25	3.4	3.25	3.4	3.15	3.4
£1,955	£1,976	£203	£1,054	£45	£781	£1,012	£938
100.6	99.3	102	98.2	102.8	95.8	103.5	96.5

Betdaq		Betonbet		Parbet		Redbet	
3.85	3.9	3.8	3.85	3.6	4	3.71	4.03
£820	£3,662	£437	£468	£1,326	£695	£1,035	£980
2.34	2.35	2.32	2.36	2.27	2.34	2.28	2.4
£13,621	£194	£200	£3	£969	£60	£956	£1,591
3.15	3.3	3.2	3.3	3	3.35	3.09	3.33
£20,886	£30	£656	£737	£1,602	£1,011	£1,005	£1,031
100.4	98.4	100.6	98.7	105.1	95.5	103.1	96.5

Betdaq		Betonbet		Parbet		Redbet	
1.94	1.96	1.94	2	—	—	—	—
£105	£160	£476	£132	—	—	—	—
4.6	4.9	4.6	4.8	—	—	—	—
£49	£169	£108	£355	—	—	—	—
3.6	3.65	3.55	3.75	—	—	—	—
£107	£23	£152	£100	—	—	—	—
101	98.8	101.3	97.5	—	—	—	—

security issues are very important.

At Betfair, all customers' funds are held in trust in a separate 'ring-fenced' account, and the same can be said for Betdaq. Betbull, who are traded on the Vienna stock exchange, also make this claim, but none of the others make it perfectly clear on their websites.

And Betonbet's terms and conditions seem to strongly suggest that it is they, and not other punters, who are matching your bets.

Here is the wording from a couple of sections of their terms and conditions:

5.4 Credit

5.4.1 The company does in no form let customers bet on credit. The accounts are dynamic, but will never let a bet be matched unless there are sufficient funds in the account. It is your responsibility to keep track of your account at any given time.

No problem here. That is exactly what you would expect from a betting exchange. But this next bit takes some explaining...

9.4 Rejection of bets

9.4.1 The company has the right to reject any bets. The bets are not valid until a customer has received a confirmation.

This is an astonishing claim for a so-called betting exchange to make. One of the biggest advantages of exchange betting is that the exchange does not care whether you win or lose, only that you bet. They take money from the winner in the form of commission. Therefore, there is no reason whatsoever for you to be refused a bet providing you have the funds in your account (as Betonbet's rule 5.4 suggests).

So Betonbet's rule 9.4.1 is surely a clear indication that they are matching your bets and that if you are a successful punter they will no longer cater for your needs.

After several attempts to contact Betonbet, I finally received a reply.

Although the firm would not confirm whether they were matching bets themselves, spokesman Tor Skeie said: "Our customers' accounts are not ring-fenced, but I can assure you that they are kept completely separate from the company's own accounts.

"We are aware that ring-fencing is an important issue for many punters in the UK especially after the incidents with, among other, Sporting Options. The reason we do not ring-fence our accounts is that we have

It is well worth mentioning that you should never completely discount the traditional bookmakers. In the match used as an example, the best draw price in the high street was 11-5, or 3.2. This is obviously worse than the 3.25 available on the exchanges, but it is better once you take into account five per cent commission (commission rates usually start at five per cent but come down depending on how much you bet). The table on page 15 shows the effect of commission on the exchange price. A bookmaker's profit margin is too big in isolation, but there is plenty of competition in the high street and quite often at least one layer's published price can be considered a viable alternative to the exchange offer.

This is especially true in lower-league football, although you tend to find that if an exchange price is shorter than available in the shops, the shop price will soon fall into line – the days of printed football coupons with unchangeable prices are numbered.

an online bank solution where it is more suitable for our business model at the moment. We pride ourselves on fast payouts and these things could become trickier with a ring-fenced set-up.

"I can also inform you that we had a complete audit of our Betting Exchange and transactions for 2004 performed by HM Customs and Excise. The result was the best references and a confirmation that the business model is sound and customers' funds are safe."

Feel free to bet with them, but the chances are if you have been closed down by the high street bookies in the UK, you will find the same happening with Betonbet.

So the two exchanges to concentrate on are Betfair and Betdaq.

Betfair has long been the largest and the big question is: is there enough room in the market for Betdaq to be a viable alternative?

There is little doubt that Betdaq, owned by Irish multi-millionaire businessman Dermot Desmond, is not going to disappear overnight owing punters a small fortune. And the exchange is clearly a competitor as far as football is concerned, but it does not compare as favourably when it comes to many other sports.

For instance, I found it quite amusing when Angus Loughran reported on BBC that a certain beaten horse had traded at 1.1 in-running with Betdaq at the Goodwood Predominate meeting in May 2005.

It may well have been true, but anyone who follows Betdaq's in-running racing markets will know that there is very little action on them.

This is because Betdaq seed several of their markets (which is not at all easy to do on an in-running horserace), something Desmond has not tried to hide. Early in 2005 he announced that he was creating a new company called Exchange Trading Strategies, in order to bypass forthcoming UK legislation which aims to prevent betting exchanges from seeding their own markets. The company operates as an autonomous legal entity from Betdaq but contributes to the liquidity on its betting markets through the placing of trades.

Of greater concern for those desperate to see a genuine competitor to Betfair is an interview Desmond gave to the *Racing Post*'s Jim Cremin early in 2005, in which he admitted that Betdaq was not profitable yet and had cost him a fortune.

Desmond is a businessman and if his venture continues to bleed, he will surely one day pull the plug.

So we come to the question of whether there is sufficient room in the marketplace for more than one exchange – and the word marketplace is quite important because an exchange is a marketplace in the first place.

Betdaq offers markedly lower commission rates yet punters still don't use it enough to make it a profitable concern. Instead, they go to Betfair because they invariably get the best prices and are assured of the liquidity that few of the firm's rivals can compete with.

They get the best prices because there is only one betting community. You can't split it in half, offer another platform and expect a completely different set of opinions and odds to arise.

Pollsters generally do a remarkably accurate job of predicting election results with samples of as few as 1,000 voters.

Betfair has an estimated 70,000 active users a week. Take half of them away and give them somewhere else to bet and the chances are you will find two exchanges with the same set of prices – but half the liquidity.

Betdaq's prices, on markets other than football, are not as competitive because the firm – or Exchange Trading Strategies – is trying to trade around their much smaller client base.

commission worries

 rates can't go too high

Fears about an increase in commission are genuine enough, but it should be noted that there is a limit as to how far Betfair could go even if they had total command of the exchange market.

For a start, Betfair remains just a small percentage of the betting market as a whole and they are never going to see off the competition from the high street firms if their charges are too high. Many firms bet to margins of just 106 per cent on several sports and when you take into account differences of opinion between bookmakers that will drop a fair bit lower, so any significant increase in commission rates would result in Betfair being uncompetitive in the global marketplace.

It is to be hoped, however, that Betdaq and any other firm with requisite financial muscle, will continue to offer some form of competition to the big cheese in the market.

This is because there is a genuine fear that total monopoly of the market will one day result in increased costs to punters via a hike in commission rates.

Betfair came under fire in April 2005 when upping their commission to seven per cent for frame-by-frame snooker markets. Many saw it as a sign of things to come.

In Betfair's defence, however, they have experimented with commission rates in many different areas and most of the changes have resulted in reductions in order to stimulate liquidity. The most notable of these was a drop to just one per cent for Asian handicaps on football in May 2005.

Betfair have made assurances that hikes in charges are not on their agenda. Things can change very quickly, though, and it's not hard to envisage a change of heart when they are floated on the stock exchange, something that will happen.

When there are shareholders to please and no competition to get in the way, even Betfair's most ardent defenders must concede that the prospect of increased charges is real.

As it stands, however, Betfair should clearly be your first port of call.

The resentment of big business is something of a tradition in Britain, yet the dynamics of exchange betting really do mean that biggest is best. ■

cantor picks up
the gauntlet

THE
SPREAD
EXCHANGE

By PAUL KEALY

A NEW TYPE OF BETTING exchange hit the market in June 2004 and unlike some which opened in direct competition with Betfair, this one looks to have a future.

Cantor Spreadfair, the exchange arm of spread betting firm Cantor Sport, launched as a football-only spread exchange in time for Euro 2004 and has quickly established itself as a popular medium among spread punters.

It rapidly expanded to take in all sports, which was always the plan, and the firm's Dominic Crosthwaite reports that Spreadfair were delighted with the way trade picked up in their first year.

He said: "We anticipated that we would attract a wide range of existing spread bettors and ex-spread bettors that no longer spread bet or had moved their betting activities on to the fixed-odds exchanges because they had been closed down.

"In addition to these clients, we have also seen excellent uptake from a broad range of Cantor Sport customers looking to trade the narrower spreads offered by Cantor Spreadfair."

Like fixed-odds exchanges, Spreadfair allows punters to bet among themselves, thus virtually eliminating the bookmakers' profit margin. There is, of course, the usual catch with commission – from a high of five per cent to a low of three per cent – charged on winnings.

That does provide a bit of a sticking point with some punters as one of the perceived major advantages of spread betting – and something much trumpeted in the early years – is that the more right you are the more you win.

The only problem here is, the more you win the more commission you pay on any single trade. Thus, if you play on a particularly volatile market – one in which the final make-up could be a long way from the initial spread – you could in theory be paying more in commission than you would had you traded at a bigger price with a traditional spread firm.

However, Crosthwaite is adamant that the reduced margins offer far greater value in the long-term for spread punters.

"Cantor Spreadfair was developed and launched in response to the fact that clients have been paying too much margin to spread betting bookmakers," he said, acknowledging that plenty of Cantor Sport punters now use Spreadfair as their spread betting medium of choice.

"There are times when the commission paid by a user on a particular market is greater than when they have traded on traditional spreads, but as this is based on significant volatility of a product, it does not happen regularly and overall as a Cantor Spreadfair user, they will be better off.

"On review of all our customers' accounts, the commission (in essence the equivalent of the bookmaker margin clients would pay traditional sports spread betting

the spread exchange

 seeding encouraged

Market seeding is often seen as a bad thing for betting exchanges to do – as some of the smaller ones could be betting with money they cannot afford to lose – but you may still be betting against Cantor's sports traders for at least some of your wagers.

This is because the Securities and Futures Authority (which polices matters relating to spread betting) wanted something in place to ensure that punters are not sucked into rank bad trades.

"The FSA requested that we maintain the integrity of the markets to ensure we minimise the risk of users of Cantor Spreadfair making trading mistakes," explained the firm's Dominic Crosthwaite.

"We are also required to monitor our markets and take great care to ensure that all clients are protected from any trading errors."

So if you want to chance your arm by offering bad value prices, Spreadfair is probably not for you.

companies) is significantly lower than the spread they would have paid.

"The unique advantage that a spread betting exchange has over a fixed-odds exchange is not only do you generally get to trade at a better price and win more if your bet is a winner, but if you lose on a spread betting exchange, you lose less as your initial trade was at a better price.

"For example, cricket, where the total runs have traditionally been traded with a spread of 20, are available for as little as one run during a game."

Liquidity in markets tends to lead to value, and already some high-profile football matches have supremacy markets that trade with a margin of as little as two-hundredths of a goal, so the signs are good that Spreadfair is here to stay.

And worries about the commission structure certainly do no appear to have surfaced given the wide range of markets now on offer.

Indeed, while Spreadfair had always intended to offer more than football, their expansion to cover all the major sports was speeded up due to punter demand.

"We knew that football would be one of our most popular sports," said Crosthwaite, "And the introduction of the new markets after Euro 2004 was based purely on client demand and closely correlated to the suitability of the product for exchange spread betting.

"Horse racing markets such as winning distances and match bets have grown very quickly, often with clients going head-to-head for large amounts. We have also seen a high level of demand for cricket, golf markets, and big sporting events such as Wimbledon or the World Snooker Championships."

Taking a profit or cutting your losses has never been more attractive for spread punters since the arrival of Spreadfair as there is little or no margin to pay for each

uncommon knowledge

competition mounts

On-course – and therefore off-course – horse racing betting margins have shrunk dramatically since Betfair became a big force and it's possibly a measure of the impact that Spreadfair has had on the spread betting industry that some of their rivals started reducing their spreads for certain markets, most notably football supremacy and total goals.

IG started the ball rolling by reducing their corners spreads from one to 0.5 in January 2005, while a week later Sporting trimmed their supremacy margin by a third to 0.2 from 0.3, did the same with total goals, and, among others things, matched IG on corners.

IG then followed by coming into line with Sporting's cuts.

Both firms denied that Spreadfair's appearance on the scene had affected trade, but they had been happy to trade with higher margins for the best part of 15 years so there must have been some reason for it.

At the time Sporting spokesman Wally Pyrah said: "We are always reviewing the size of our spreads and feel we need to continue giving significant value to maintain our leading position in the marketplace."

Cantor's Graham Cowdrey took an understandably more bullish stance, saying: "They are offering tighter spreads because they realise they are unable to compete with us in delivering what every punter demands – value."

Whatever the case, it was good news for spread punters in general, and though realistically Spreadfair has a long way to go before challenging Sporting and IG for market supremacy, their rivals' reactions suggest they are at least alive to the threat.

---

end of the bet. And Spreadfair expect to see a good many more traders once they have the software in place (it wasn't by July 2005) to allow punters to put up bids and offers simultaneously.

"We are seeing a steady increase in number of clients carrying out pure trading and expect with the addition of a pure trading tool to see this increase significantly," said Crosthwaite.

"A good example of a market where Cantor Spreadfair clients trade in and out a lot more frequently than they would with a traditional spread firm is cricket runs.

"If a client expects a team quoted 280-300 with a spread firm to start well enough to earn a future quote around 300-320, but then finally end up around 300, they are unlikely to have a bet as they would have to pay 40 runs worth of

Premiership Points 2005-2006	So Far	Available to Sell			Available to Buy		
				Best Bid	Best Offer		
Arsenal		78.1	78.2	78.3	78.5	78.6	78.7
		£200	£300	£828	£250	£300	£25
Aston Villa		49.3	49.4	49.5	49.7	49.9	50.2
		£80	£200	£165	£401	£200	£491
Birmingham		46.4	47.0	47.1	47.4	47.5	47.7
		£68	£300	£172	£25	£240	£430
Blackburn		45.4	45.5	45.6	45.8	46.1	46.4
		£50	£300	£300	£15	£500	£117
Bolton		49.0	49.1	49.2	49.4	49.5	49.6
		£400	£207	£250	£50	£475	£1400
Charlton		46.0	46.1	46.2	46.7	46.8	47.1
		£561	£940	£64	£132	£439	£681
Chelsea		85.9	86.0	86.4	86.6	86.7	86.8
		£400	£20	£124	£100	£918	£200

How Spreadfair's Premiership points markets looked in July 2005

margin and neither price gives an opportunity to profit.

"On Cantor Spreadfair they might be able to buy at 290 and then not only close their buy position at 310 but also take a new sell position."

As with Betfair, it makes little difference to Spreadfair whether punters are winners or losers – they never close winning accounts – so Crosthwaite had no qualms about offering trading advice.

"The first thing customers should think about is what their objectives are," he said.

"Are they looking for a fun interest on some televised sport, a challenge to trade against the market and test their knowledge, or with an aim to make profit?

"A conservative approach is to look for arbitrage opportunities between Cantor Spreadfair and other spread firms, exchanges or fixed-odds bookmakers. These will always exist and, unlike with traditional bookmakers and spread firms, exchanges welcome arbitrage players as they are great for liquidity and allow big-hitting clients to get matched when they want to take strong positions against the market.

"Other successful punters often focus on one or two sports where they can build up expert knowledge, or use statistical analysis to attempt to gain an advantage over the market prices.

"Traders often look to trade in and out near the middle of the spread on the stronger markets, looking at the weight of money and market momentum to judge which way to open their position and then aim to quickly close out for a small profit." ■

no substitute for knowledge

RACING

By MATT
WILLIAMS

YOU HAVE PRESUMABLY bought this book to learn about betting on exchanges. Well, you are on to a winner as there is no better way to gamble. Exchanges lead the way in every respect. Percentages, value, choice and fun – the most underrated ingredient on the exchanges – are there at your fingertips.

Don't be unnerved by sensationalist claims of increased corruption in racing, caused by the supposed nuisance that is betting exchanges.

The likelihood is you may at some point get caught up in the swindle of a classic racing caper, but that is one of the downsides we as gamblers have learned to deal with over the years. Little has changed and, if anything, the exchanges will lead to something being done about it.

There is more than one way to skin a cat, and backing and laying is not the be all and end all of exchange betting. Yes, the whole concept of a person-to-person betting site is built on a 'I want to back X at Y/I want to lay X at Y' foundation, but the industry has developed and evolved into something much more diverse, so much so that there are any number of ways to make good money on a betting exchange nowadays.

IN-RUNNING STRATEGY Fortunately, I have been able to make a decent living on the exchanges since their conception, and I suppose if I analysed exactly where my strengths lay, the answer would be my skill to pinpoint value after the tapes have risen or the gates have opened. The cynics will say that I make the most of my position as a columnist for the *Racing Post*, getting the most out of the SIS feed that we have wired through to the office. My reply is that the cynics are talking complete nonsense.

Granted, the time delays in the early days, concerning At The Races and SIS, could have been beneficial, but I don't believe those who think there are scores of people driving around in flash cars on account of having access to a super-fast feed.

There is no doubting, though, that there is a time delay and much depends on what platform you are watching from.

For instance, both digitial and cable TV are slower than terrestrial TV, so if you are watching RUK or At The Races when Channel 4 or BBC is an option you really should switch over.

And judging by some of the late bets struck, it appears that many people do not.

Terrestrial TV is faster even than SIS, but not by a massive margin. However, it has been known to be up to three seconds faster than cable and we are talking about around 60 yards here.

But in my experience, there is no substitute for knowledge. Get to know your colours and your horses. Learn about running styles – it's a big advantage to know which horses don't stay, or which horses will be running on late in the day.

List-compilers will tell you to make a note of everything that catches your attention, be it a horse to swerve next time out, or an unlucky in-running beast which is sure to win its next race. It's a system I don't follow myself, but I can see its uses, and wouldn't put anyone off a trip to W H Smith to buy some notebooks and pencils – I'm too lazy.

In-running betting is not as easy as just picking out the horse that is travelling best a furlong out. We all have eyes, and we can

finding your feet

 start with small stakes

Time delays aside, there are a lot of considerations to take on board with the in-running markets before you go swimming with the sharks. If you don't know your form, you'll quickly lose what bank you have and, as harsh as it may seem, you deserve what is coming your way. I'd like to think there are punters reading this who have a tremendous grasp of the formbook, but are just too set in their ways to take the online plunge.

But you don't have to go all-in straight away. In fact, you should find your feet with small stakes as you explore the different betting mediums, and work out which strategy best suits your individual punting style.

become a
pace ace

 a lesson learned

Never has the importance of pace been so well conveyed to the public than on Oaks day 2005 when the *Racing Post*'s James Willoughby compared the running of the Oaks with that of the Coronation Cup on Racing UK.

With RUK showing both races simultaneously on a split screen, we could see that the pace winner Yeats set in the Coronation Cup was much slower – something like five seconds at halfway – than that being set in the Oaks.

What it showed was that Yeats was running well within itself and was able to keep up a gallop for much longer, while those up with the pace in the Oaks were going too fast and would tire. Yeats never saw another horse and galloped home 2.5 lengths clear in a time 2.02secs faster than eventual Oaks winner Eswarah. The Oaks pacesetters paid the price for their suicidal tactics, with the first five horses returning with the *Racing Post* comment 'settled in midfield' or 'held up'. This invaluable lesson was worth the RUK subscription fee on its own.

all see which horse is cruising. The art of becoming a successful in-running bettor revolves entirely around being able to predict the unpredictable.

If you start backing the obvious at ludicrously short prices you will soon start to feel it in your pocket. Remember, the first thing you see is likely be the first thing everyone else sees and the mad clamour to back or lay will result in some shocking prices being offered and taken.

Try to visualise how you think a race will develop – if you get it right, you'll be in a great position to close out a winning trade.

If the authorities ever introduce sectional timing to our racing, I believe in-running betting will go crazy. It will work best on consistent tracks, like Lingfield's all-weather course, but trying to make the correct call around Carlisle on a soggy Monday would be complete guesswork. Anyway, without the obvious benefits of sectionals, punters would do well to learn as much as they can about pace.

You only have to watch the racing in the US to know how important pace is, when even a moderate judge will be able to tell you if a horse will last out the trip, or if they are going too slow. They don't need a clock to tell you, either, they just know.

However, if you visited a betting establishment in England most of the customers would give you a blank look if you questioned them about sectional timing. Get to know what a fast pace looks like, and a slow one, as they are both of equal importance. You will only get the hang of pace by watching as much racing as you can.

JOCKEYS Certain jockeys have the ability to make a horse travel like a 1.1 shot at the furlong marker, while others employ a more industrious riding style, thus forcing a price to stand up, as online punters believe his or her mount has nothing left to give. I'll give you three examples of a bridle

Kieren Fallon rode a great race from the front on Yeats in the 2005 Coronation Cup at Epsom

jockey (there is no significance in the order) from the Flat and National Hunt scenes.

FLAT
1. Jamie Spencer
2. Richard Hughes
3. George Baker

NH
1. Timmy Murphy
2. Paul Carberry
3. Ruby Walsh

It's no coincidence that five of the six jockeys listed are Irish. These boys have been brought up riding horses on soft ground – conditions in which quiet riders do particularly well.

Knowing your horses will obviously help when assessing charges ridden by these boys as many times it will be the runners that look like they are poised to strike that will be the ones with nothing left in the tank – or who are not prepared to use what's left. And many times they will be

Hardy Eustace (right) and Harchibald (centre) fight out the Champion Hurdle finish in 2005

traded at ludicrously short prices as the mugs fall over themselves to get on. Find a bridle horse with a bridle jockey and the chances are you are sitting on a goldmine.

FRONT RUNNERS Common sense tells you a front-runner will almost always shorten once it gets its favoured position in a race. Anything that steals a long lead virtually always gets backed down to a false price and that includes pre-race no-hopers.

However, at which point should the trader jump ship by laying it back? Like a lot of factors on the exchanges, it is entirely up to the individual, and there is no right or wrong answer to this question. But once a front runner tires, it tends to do so dramatically and if you leave it too late you will be stuck with a losing bet.

BLANKET LAYING IN-RUNNING This is not something I get involved in myself, but many people obviously do.

If you are looking for an idea of how the market moves when betting in-running,

uncommon knowledge

in-running layers
wise up to Harchibald

One of the most famous examples of a bridle horse/jockey partnership must be that of Harchibald and Paul Carberry, although in-running punters seemed to have latched on to them by the time of the 2005 Champion Hurdle.

Carberry had Harchibald running all over Hardy Eustace after the last flight of hurdles and seemingly all he needed to do was press the button to win cheekily. Yet when Harchibald was asked for the final surge in the last 50 yards, he found nothing, and Hardy Eustace won by a neck.

Had this race been run at a gaffe track like Fakenham between two lesser known horses, Harchibald would almost certainly have hit 1.10 and possibly gone shorter but because this animal's quirks were known by all and sundry, he hit only 1.25 in running.

Nevertheless, Carberry was roundly slated by punters for failing to ask his mount for his effort earlier in the race and he probably still hasn't been forgiven by some despite Harchibald again being beaten next time in the Emo Oil Champion Hurdle at Punchestown. This time he had been rousted along immediately after jumping the last, but found nil when Brave Inca – behind him at Cheltenham – fought back.

you could learn plenty from writing down all the pre-race prices and then comparing them with the lowest price that has been matched in-running.

Sometimes it's not easy to work out, but the graph on each horse's price history (click on the horse's name and it will pop up in a new window) will give you a fair idea. What you will see is that many horses – not just the front runners – are matched at much lower prices during a race, even if, to your eyes, they never really looked like winning.

And you will also spot that on several occasions more than one horse (sometimes three) will have been matched at odds-on.

Different people see different things and some punters take advantage by putting up prices straight after the off.

If you watch for the market to reopen after the off, the first thing you are likely to see is a raft of prices at odds-on offered about all the runners.

What the layer is hoping to do is get at least two runners matched. Sometimes

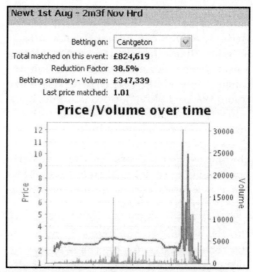

Newt 1st Aug – 2m3f Nov Hrd

Betting on: Cantgeton

Total matched on this event: **£824,619**
Reduction Factor **38.5%**
Betting summary - Volume: **£347,339**
Last price matched: **1.01**

Price/Volume over time

The price history for Cantgeton in a novice hurdle at Newton Abbot. The evens favourite came up against a 'bridle' horse and subsequently drifted out to 12 before his price collapsed again as his rival found nothing

they will lose, but many times they will win and there most be something in it, at least for certain races, otherwise people would not consistently offer to cover the field.

COURSE GUIDES Philip Robinson has a reputation for always being one step ahead of his weighing-room colleagues, and does things like walking the course before racing and finding out any details in relation to any given day's racing from course officials.

A lot of jockeys walk the course, but Robinson makes it his business to find out where the best ground is and he's always looking to find an unconventional route to the winning post. Exchange punters can learn a lot from Robinson's meticulous approach, and by adapting a similar method to our online activities we could all become better punters.

Listed over the next few pages is a brief guide to each of the 59 courses in the Britain. As you can imagine, some offer a lot more than others in terms of providing a useful edge. For example a dodgy photo-finish angle could result in a six-figure trade. We are talking serious numbers here.

First, though, here are a couple of general points that may help. There is a draw bias at many tracks but the bias can change over the years, so there is little point in being really forthright here unless there is a longstanding historical advantage (ie. tracks such as Beverley).

The best way to keep up to date with the draw bias at any track is by using the results search for big races at racing-post.co.uk. Those who like trends will also be able to pick up on other pointers before reading them in the *Racing Post* on big race days.

However, it is not unknown for courses to mess about with the stalls positions without making such movements public and they will often render any draw bias meaningless.

This sort of information is vital for punters but many course executives seem to have little regard for us and we usually only find out after the opener is won by some unconsidered 50-1 poke (as hap-pened when The Jobber won a Sandown sprint from the percieved 'coffin' draw in July 2005). So the way to hit back is to give the clerks of the course a ring on racedays to establish that the stalls posi-tions have been correctly conveyed to the press.

If enough of us pester them on a regular basis they will not dream of making changes without doing their best to make sure every-one knows well in advance and the *Racing Post* will always publish such information.

AINTREE The fences on the Mildmay Course are quite stiff and can take plenty

Aintree's Mildmay course fences are among the stiffest in the country

of jumping. Suits a handy type of horse, with most big chases being won by those up with the pace. However, big-field hurdles are usually won from off the pace.

After trading on Hedgehunter's 2005 Grand National, I reached the conclusion that in-running betting on the greatest of all great races is the business. Don't try to be too clever by telling yourself to be patient, or waiting until they go out on the second circuit. You're a punter, not a jockey.

I found that all of my fancies (three of them) were trading shorter than the pre-race odds early on, especially Clan Royal, who touched around 2-1 before unseating Tony McCoy at Becher's second time round. It stands to reason that the opposite may be true with an outsider, so if you fancy a 33-1 chance feel free to wait.

Course pointer: concentrate your attentions on piecing together a Grand National portfolio in the months before the race, as prices collapse once the weights are announced.

ASCOT (DUE TO RE-OPEN IN 2006)
Small fields are the norm for National Hunt meetings, so in-running carnage is something of a rarity. The Flat course is very fair, but it's always worth studying the big-field draw bias.
Course pointer: the track has put down new turf, which will take some bedding down, and I expect there will be various advantages (with the ground) and disadvantages (with the draw) when it re-opens.

AYR Flat and National Hunt courses are both very fair, but sprint fields tend to split when numbers are high, and draw bias exists.
Course pointer: William Haggas and Barry Hills do well with their runners at the big Western meeting, especially with their well-backed contenders.

BANGOR ON DEE Bangor is a little gem of a track. In-running punters have made a killing by siding with the pace, and Bangor is to jump racing what Chester is to Flat racing – the front-runner has that big an edge.
Course pointer: like I've already said, back the pace, you won't go far wrong.

BATH One of the great myths is the supposed inside-draw bias in sprint races. High numbers actually have a good record, and you should never dismiss one because it's drawn 14 of 14.
Course pointer: watch out for runners arriving wide, late and fast. The description fits many a winner, meeting after meeting.

BEVERLEY Occasionally, the course executives take it upon themselves to try to mess with the well-established high-draw bias, so never take stalls position for granted.

in-running options

 explaining back-to-lay

There are two separate back-to-lay strategies worth considering. First, you may think a horse is a value bet at the odds and be pretty sure that it will trade at shorter odds in-running, in which case you can cover your stake by giving a bit back.

Secondly, you may fancy a horse getting beat but can see it trading at a very short price. In this case you can back it at pre-race odds and then take a chunk out of it in-running.

I know several punters who made hay by doing this with Rooster Booster throughout the 2004-05 NH campaign.

You could argue that an in-running lay would suffice, but every now and again you are going to lay an odds-on winner, so if you can do so without any cost involved, so much the better.

Decide how low you wish to go and get your order up early is the advice.

Course pointer: don't be fooled into thinking the draw bias is limited to sprint distances – it isn't.

BRIGHTON Speed is a vital ingredient for success around one of Britain's most bizarre venues. People talk about the downhill run at Epsom, but it has nothing on Brighton.

Course pointer: stiff uphill finish inside the final furlong has caused many a 1.1 shot to get chinned – fast finishers do well here.

CARLISLE Heavy-ground horses do well during the winter – a time of the year when stamina is at a premium.

Course pointer: don't take anything for granted around here, as horses tend to tire badly when meeting the stiff uphill finish.

CARTMEL A novelty track if ever there was one. Suits a front-runner and you don't often see horses coming from a long way back to win.

Course pointer: the run-in seems to last forever, and sometimes jockeys ride an ill-judged race by sending on their mounts too far from home.

CATTERICK High draw is rarely a positive around here in big fields, and whether it's a five-furlong dash or a two-mile handicap, you are normally better off siding with those drawn middle to low

Course pointer: in-running punters can take advantage of anything that gets to the front on an easy lead – they usually stay there.

CHELTENHAM The fences are stiff, and the climb to the winning post lends itself to dramatic last-gasp finishes.

Cross-country racing is now a feature at the Festival meeting, and deserves a mention. The 3m7f trip is not as big an influence on stamina as you might imagine,

The uphill climb at Cheltenham gives rise to many dramatic finishes

as they tend to go steady for a long way, and you often see a sprint finish.

Course pointer: it often pays to follow the hold-up types and it takes a special effort to win from the front.

CHEPSTOW Stamina is a big issue when the going is soft. However, the home straight is all downhill, which tends to favour a front-runner, and a high percentage of winners are either making the pace or are up with it.

Course pointer: on the flat the general rule is to go for horses drawn middle-to-high.

CHESTER This place is like a bull ring, and the horses are on the turn virtually throughout. It's a well known fact that you need to be drawn low in five and six furlong sprint races, so much so trainers are prone to withdraw their runners if they are burdened with an outside draw.

Course pointer: while low numbers are the rage for the short sprints, seven furlong races (with 12 plus runners) actually throw up a number of successes for high draws.

DONCASTER Years ago Doncaster's fences were thought to be among the easiest in the country. However, a large number of fallers in the last couple of seasons have put the record straight, and you need a safe jumper. The sweeping bends and long home straight benefit the long-striding galloper on the Flat course.

Course pointer: pay attention to the Lincoln meeting in March, as it's a time of the year when the bookies are in the dark with regard to the draw, ground, etc.

EPSOM A great course for the speed merchants. They do especially well when allowed to travel at a steady pace in the lead. My earlier reference to sectionals, and realising what a slow (or fast) pace looks like can pay dividends. If a situation arises when a horse is allowed to dictate its own fractions, the better in-running judges will make a killing. They know the leader is almost certainly going to be there or thereabouts at the finish, and are therefore able to trade a win-win position.

Course pointer: middle-distance races can change quickly when they meet the rising ground, and it often pays to concentrate your in-running attentions on a finisher.

EXETER Tony McCoy galvanised Mini Sensation to win a staying handicap chase around here at in-running odds of 1,000. This bet only materialised because of the stiff uphill climb to the finish, when stamina is always at a premium.

Course pointer: you won't go far wrong by following the top boys like Martin Pipe and Philip Hobbs. In-running punters should always be prepared for rapidly changing positions up the home straight and plenty of 1.0-somethings get chinned on the run-in, which is surprising when you consider how short it is.

FAKENHAM Very sharp and similar to Cartmel in many respects – it's a speedster's track where exaggerated hold-up tactics rarely do well.
Course pointer: a course specialists' track so follow those with regular good form there.

FOLKESTONE High numbers tend to do well in the sprint races, and it is not unusual to see the field heading for the far side rail, even in a five-runner scenario.
Course pointer: everything about this gaff track is bland, and the in-running action isn't up to much, either.

FONTWELL Suits a front-runner, and an ideal place to send a dodgy jumper, as the fences are quite soft and you often see horses jumping straight through them without coming down.
Course pointer: uphill climb after the last can cause a horse to weaken, and veer under pressure.

GOODWOOD High numbers are favoured on the round course, and the same rule applies to larger fields in the sprint races on the straight course, although it's always worth checking out recent stats.
Course pointer: the in-running action is always top-class, with horses getting into all sorts of trouble on the rail, as they struggle for room.

HAMILTON The famous high-draw bias exists on soft/heavy ground, but on fast going the spread of winners is more even.
Course pointer: don't be fooled into thinking a horse is out of it as it comes under pressure running downhill entering the home straight, because some tend to run on again as they meet the rising ground.

HAYDOCK Very fair track, and although the fences are big and stiff, they are considered among the best in the country.

in-running options

 explaining lay-to-back

Not all horses quicken up immediately to win races and if you can spot something that responds to pressure before other punters latch on to it a lay-to-back play could be the call.

You will be amazed at how quickly horses drift once they come under pressure, but while with some it's a sure sign they are weakening, with others they are just starting to get going.

The inititial lay can save you any losses if the horse does get beat, while sometimes you will get some stunning prices during the race for a free bet.

Course pointer: there used to be a definite high-draw bias in the soft-ground sprints. However, recent results suggest the middle of the course is the place to be, as always with the draw, though, things change and it often pays to be on the ball.

HEREFORD With just one fence/hurdle up the home straight, you often see jockeys riding a finish a long way from home, which sometimes causes in-running panic.
Course pointer: a great track for horses racing up with the pace, and course specialists have a good record (obviously, but you know what I mean).

HEXHAM This gaff is a graveyard for front-runners, and because of its stamina-sapping hills, the hold-up types have a great record.
Course pointer: despite the stiff nature of the track, some jockeys go for home far too early and many runners tire dramatically after the last. It's very changeable.

HUNTINGDON A sharp track, with easy fences, there is little or no edge to be gained by trawling through past results – it's a very fair track.
Course pointer: with the emphasis on speed, ex-flat horses do well over hurdles.

KELSO What an arse of a camera angle this place has, and meeting after meeting produces some sort of in-running/photo finish disaster.
Course pointer: because of the iffy camera angle, photo-finish betting is something of a lottery, and I wouldn't take anything for granted, so don't try to buy money on a 1.1 shot in the photo markets.

KEMPTON Flat and National Hunt courses place emphasis on speed, and you should be looking for a handy type that has the ability to quicken – plodders just don't win around here. New all-weather Flat track due to open in 2006.

Course pointer: watch out for the first fence up the home straight, as it has a nasty habit of catching horses out.

LEICESTER A very fair track with no real biases.

Course pointer: has its share of undulations, and is a lot stiffer than it appears on the box.

LINGFIELD This is a notoriously difficult place to make all the running in sprint races on turf and all-weather tracks.

Course pointer: the exact opposite is true for the middle-distance and staying races on the turf track, when a front-runner is often difficult to peg back.

LUDLOW Soft-ground horses usually struggle, as the course drains exceptionally well and it's a rarity to see the going worsen beyond good to soft.

Course pointer:: beware the four tricky (not stiff or overly difficult) fences up the home straight. Tired animals have been known to make costly errors over them.

MARKET RASEN A sharp track on which course specialists have a particularly good record. Local trainer Michael Chapman has a habit of unearthing double-digit winners.

Course pointer:: front-runners have a tremendous record in small fields.

MUSSELBURGH A low draw in big fields on the round course can cause problems, as the bends are sharp (you see more horses running wide here than any other track in my opinion).

Course pointer: they tend to go flat out in sprints. Lately, races over seven furlongs and a mile have been run at too fast a pace, which has led to an increased number of hold-up performers doing well.

wbury is one of the country's fairest tracks

NEWBURY One of the fairest venues in Britain, over jumps and on the level.
Course pointer: races up to a mile on the straight track are not as easy as you'd imagine, and stamina is often an issue in the closing stages – horses do tire.

NEWCASTLE A notoriously difficult place to make all the running and camera angle is right up there with Kelso, throwing every photo-finish into crazy uncertainty.
Course pointer: watch how the camera focuses in on the apparent winner about 50 yards from the line, only to pan out into a wider focus. Early in-running bettors used to get caught out by this (1.01s should have been 1.1s), but most of us are wise to it now.

NEWMARKET A well-known draw nut tells me there is no bias at Newmarket, but I disagree. In big fields, high numbers (in races up to a mile) have done better than those drawn low in recent years.
Course pointer: front-runners are difficult to chase down on fast ground on both July and Rowley courses.

NEWTON ABBOT Races are farmed by the West Country mafia (Pipe, Nicholls and Hobbs), and the in-running action is often poor to say the least.
Course pointer: if your selection jumps the final fence with a lead of a length or more go and collect.

NOTTINGHAM Draw bias tends to vary on the straight course, and a lot depends on what is happening with the weather, but high draw is always difficult to overcome on the round course in big fields.
Course pointer: the strip of ground right by the far rail is often worth a length or two on the round course.

PERTH The camera is always miles away from the action at Perth, and I've been caught out many a time by backing (or laying) a certain horse which appears to be a couple of lengths clear approaching the second-last only to jump level.
Course pointer: it's behind Kelso and New-castle for awkward photo's, but still iffy.

PONTEFRACT Stiff uphill finish places emphasis on stamina, and whereas non-stayers can get away with their shortcomings at places like Kempton, they are always found out around here.
Course pointer: the perceived low-draw bias in sprints is nowhere near as strong as some would have you believe.

PLUMPTON They usually get well strung out around here, the main reason being the jockeys seem to get after their mounts a lot earlier than usual.
Course pointer: soft ground usually features through the dire winter months, and tired horses can stop in front – something you tend to see more on the hurdles course.

REDCAR If situated in a more fashionable

part of the country Redcar would be a lot more popular because it is flat and fair.

Course pointer: suits the speedier types and you get a lot of close finishes.

RIPON The draw on the straight course is always a major factor in determining a bias (can change from meeting to meeting), as is the draw on the round course, which has a definite leaning to those drawn high.

Course pointer: in-running punters love to follow a front-runner blindly on the round course, with the main ingredient including a high draw to get the favoured rail. They often stay clear of their field.

SALISBURY There is often in-running chaos, a high-draw is usually favoured on the round course but soft ground causes a tremendous amount of indecision, with runners often spread all over the track.

Course pointer: this is one of my favourite in-running tracks. The downhill run into the home straight gives the impression a front-runner is full of running, and when they kick for home the visual impression is usually misleading, as they still have a climb to negotiate before the winning post – a lot can happen inside the final furlong.

SANDOWN The chase course presents a stiff test, even for the better jumpers, and you rarely have a situation where a dodgy jumper wins around Sandown.

Course pointer: with its stiff uphill finish, Sandown is up there with Cheltenham for its high-profile final-furlong turnarounds – always be on the lookout for a finisher.

SEDGEFIELD Left-handed gaff, with sharp bends that stages consistently poor-quality racing.

Course pointer: often unwise to get too far behind early even over longer distances. The fences are among the easiest in the country.

SOUTHWELL The chase course is vile, and I rarely get too involved on account of the high number of fallers. The all-weather track (with deep sand making it similar to soft going on the turf) provides a much better vehicle for punters.
Course pointer: it's hard for hold-up horses to win, especially if they stay to the inside of the course. And pay attention to whatever travels on the bridle rounding the home turn; if they have no stamina issues, they normally win.

STRATFORD Can't enthuse about this place, except to say the photo-finish angle is not the easiest.
Course pointer: the sharp nature of the course often leads to a too-fast pace and many odds-on shots can get turned over after turning in with a healthy lead over fences.

TAUNTON Sharp track which usually attracts poor quality racing.
Course pointer: a flat track with the emphasis on speed so look to Flat-bred types in novice hurdles.

THIRSK Front-runners have done really well in recent seasons on fast ground, but always oppose a front-runner in-running on soft ground.
Course pointer: no obvious bias in sprint races, but it pays to note earlier races on any given card.

TOWCESTER When the going gets heavy, I would say Towcester is the most stamina-dependent track in Britain. The stiff uphill finish makes Cheltenham look tame, and the in-running action is sometimes so crazy you'd struggle to write the script.
Course pointer: anyone backing odds-on around here is taking a big risk, as the course lends itself perfectly to upsets.

uncommon knowledge

 following the money

Following gambles is a sure way to the poorhouse and always has been. Join the gamble at the last moment and you are on at the worst price and if you consistently take poor value you will lose in the long run, no matter how informed the gamble is.

In 2005 Betfair commissioned a study of 2,000 races from the last six months of 2004 in a bid to counteract allegations that exchanges pose a threat to racing's integrity, with non-triers allegedly being laid and drifting out massively in price.

What they discovered was that punters would have been far better off backing the drifters than those whose price shortened – the level stakes profit was 570 points for drifters, with a 345-point loss shown for shorteners.

A drifter was defined as a horse whose price had moved out a minimum 20 per cent in the five minutes leading up to a race, while for a shortener the reverse was true.

Of course, many gambles are landed, so to say you should completely ignore all of them is too simplistic.

We probably all have our lists of trainers to follow when the money is down and those to avoid.

This is very much a personal choice but my favourites to follow would be Willie Haggas, Peter Chapple-Hyam, Mark Wallace and the Easterbys, while I would always be keen to lay talking horses from the big stables – Stoute, O'Brien, etc – and would take on anything short from the Charlie Mann stable.

UTTOXETER Very fair, and doesn't take much rain, so going gets desperately sticky at times.
Course pointer:: photo-finishes are difficult to call.

WARWICK Fences come thick and fast down the back straight, and poor jumpers are often left with too much to do if they have an off day. On the Flat, it is also a tough track for inexperienced two-year-olds on account of the sharp bend at the top of the home straight.
Course pointer: in-running punters should back front-runners blindly when they are allowed to bowl along with an easy lead. This only applies on fast ground, though.

WETHERBY Genuine bridle course, and anything that looks in trouble usually stays in trouble.
Course pointer: you need to judge the pace

around here, as it is hard to come from a long way back unless the leaders have gone really hard.

WINCANTON One of the easiest tracks in the country, and speed horses generally have the upper hand.
Course pointer: Paul Nicholls enjoys loads of success at his local course, and a lot of markets usually revolve around his horses.

WINDSOR I find Windsor one of the most difficult venues to play in-running. The track layout throws up awkward angles, and the eye can play tricks on you, which is never a good thing when split-second decisions have to be made.
Course pointer: front-runners that grab the stands' side rail on fast ground usually take some passing.

WOLVERHAMPTON Front-runners fared best soon after the polytrack replaced the old fibresand surface. However, things are more even these days.
Course pointer: perfect in-running course for good pace judges, as those who get the fractions right usually come out on top.

WORCESTER Quite sharp, so you would think pace horses would thrive by getting away from their field. But this couldn't be further from the truth, and Evan Williams sent out two massive in-running horses in the summer of 2005, one trading at 1,000.
Course pointer: a long straight, and I wouldn't normally be in a rush to put all my eggs in one basket early doors.

YARMOUTH Very popular with Newmarket trainers, and Godolphin have been known to send one of their better two-year-olds there for its debut. Draw can play its part on the straight course, but generally perceived to be a fair track

Course pointer: Christine Dunnett likes to train winners here, and she seems to have big-price successes every year.

YORK Hold-up horses should be avoided in sprints, and those drawn in extremes normally struggle as the winner almost always races up the middle. Anything held up on fast ground is on a hiding to nothing. *Course pointer:* long gone are the days when a high draw meant curtains. Class can overcome most things at York, except giving away a distance of ground on fast going.

GETTING ON EARLY Betfair put their day-of-race markets up at around 8pm the night before racing and this is the time when you could sneak a bit of value.

The first shows that appear on Betfair are invariably similar to the tissue price provided on the *Racing Post*'s website, racingpost.co.uk, and while I in no way wish to criticise my colleagues, the spotlight writers are under instense time pressure.

It is to their credit that betting forecasts are so remarkably accurate most of the time but, as in any walk of life, mistakes are sometimes made. And if you think you have spotted one – or even a potential gamble that you fancy to develop – asking for prices overnight could prove beneficial.

This is not exactly a big-hitters' domain, though, as it is always wise to be cautious when asking for prices. If you put up a big chunk and are right, the chances are you have just alerted everyone. And if you are badly wrong, your stake will be swallowed up and you will be stuck with a poor value bet. But to small stakes you can often pinch way over the odds.

TAKING ON THE LAYERS Many bookmakers hold their prices in the betting shops on big race days until 10.15am to allow regular cash punters the chance to get the best price available.

However, I can see the day coming that the bookies pull the plug and the reason, quite simply, is arbitrage.

The layers are already changing football coupon prices in shops if there is an arbitrage due to a gamble on Betfair and something similar looks sure to happen in racing at some stage.

At the moment, though, people prepared to make the effort to pick up some free money – or at worst a free bet – can take advantage of this bookmaker generosity.

Several firms hold their prices on races that feature in the *Racing Post*'s Pricewise column, even though the Pricewise selection – and those of some of the more reputable tippping lines – tends to be heavily backed.

And with Betfair's day-of-race markets available for trading the night before, what you often see is a huge wad of money requesting to back a horse at much shorter than what is on offer at your local bookies.

And all you need to do is lay that and then nip down to the bookies in question and take the bigger price.

Make sure, though, that you know in advance how much the layer is prepared to let you have as some firms have more stringent limits than others. You won't win fortunes in one go doing this, but one thing is certain, you will never lose – until the layers call it a day and stop the fun.

Here is another way of picking off the old enemy. I don't know what it is about some bookmakers, but judging by some of their decisions their hatred of betting exchanges-must mean they don't even bother to see how the market is forming.

Take Ladbrokes, for example. They commendably try to spice up the day-by-day racing fare by offering individual match bets on many races, quoting horses at 5-6 each of two or, in some cases 4-6 and 11-10.

But when framing these markets, they don't seem to be giving the morning and early-afternoon Betfair market – probably the most accurate tissue in the industry – any credence at all.

What this means is that sometimes horses that appear evenly-matched to the Ladbrokes odds-compilers are priced much differently in the outright race market on Betfair. Indeed, I have seen horses trading at 10 and 36 being offered at 5-6 each of two in a match by Ladbrokes. That's an extreme example but you will often see a gap of several points.

It doesn't take a genius to work out that by backing the shorter one at 5-6 in the match you are getting terrific market value, but here is the really good bit. When it comes to the opening show at the course, if there is similar difference in prices, which more often than not there is, Ladbrokes can no longer justify going each of two. In many cases they will be forced to bet 1-2 and 6-4, while sometimes they will have to go even shorter about the favourite.

So all you need is two accounts with Ladbrokes on the internet – which is not hard to do nowadays, just get someone else to come in with you – and you can now back the underdog and guarantee yourself a profit whichever one wins.

Let's not get carried away, though. You won't be able to get massive bets on for long (if at all) and if you start becoming remotely successful you will soon be limited to ridiculous stakes or closed down completely.

That's why exchanges are king. ■

betting when the price is right

FOOTBALL

Celtic celebrate winning the European Cup in 1967

"I'LL KICK EVERY BALL TONIGHT. I'll go through the game, over and over again. I can see everybody's face. I can see their build. I can see the way they run. You should be the same, thinking out all the possibilities."

By KEVIN PULLEIN

So said Jock Stein, manager of Celtic when they became the first British club to win the European Cup. He was not speaking to bettors, but his words still apply to us. We should be the same.

The possibilities that interest us may not be exactly the same as those that interested him, but we should think about them beforehand just as thoroughly.

If the game is still scoreless after, say, an hour, what are the chances that there will be a goal? If the favourites should then take the lead, what are the chances that the outsiders will be able to fight back and get an equaliser – or that the favourites will be able to hold them off and perhaps even build a bigger advantage? At the final whistle, how many goals will there be?

We should try to anticipate as many possibilities as we can, and ask ourselves how each of them should affect the odds in the various markets that are traded in-play on the betting exchanges.

Because there won't be time during the game. And the lack of time puts us under pressure, which can do funny things to our judgement.

We should not reach inflexible conclusions – because, on occasions, we will find ourselves watching a match that is completely different from the one for which we prepared.

It happened, incidentally, to Stein in the 1970 European Cup final – three years after Celtic's glorious triumph over Inter – when he discovered to his horror that Feyenoord were a very different and much better team than he had realised on his scouting trip to Holland.

Yet, most of the time, the match for which we prepare will be, pretty much, the one the players produce.

The basic principles of football betting are the same before and during a game. The most basic principle of all is this: that we can only win money, in the long run, if we bet on events that are more likely to occur than the odds imply – if our prospects of winning are greater than is implied by our prospective winnings.

In a chapter in an earlier book in this series, *The Definitive Guide to Betting on Sport*, I discussed ways of estimating what the odds should be on a variety of events in a match at the moment it begins. Over the next few pages, I will describe how I believe those odds should change once it has begun, as the action unfolds.

COMMISSION First, though, I think I should say a few words on commission.

The price you see on the screen – the price at which your bet will supposedly be settled – is not the price at which your bet will actually be settled.

Because, on an exchange, you pay up to five per cent of your profit from winning bets to the operator. It's how they make their profit.

You should always allow for – and never underestimate – the impact of commission. It can be dramatic.

Suppose you think that the true odds about a team winning at this moment in a match are evens – 2.0 in decimals, which is what we shall use from now on. And that you are right to do so.

If you pay five per cent commission, you will have to be able to back this team at more than 2.05 or lay them at 1.95 just to get a fair bet – that is, to be paid out at 2.0 if your bet should be successful.

But we don't want a fair bet. We can only win money, in the long run, with unfair bets – that is to say, bets which are unfair to the people we are betting with.

So let's suppose that you set yourself a target of making five per cent profit on your betting turnover. Just five per cent.

If you pay five per cent commission and want to make five per cent profit on turnover, what odds will you need to be able to get about this team whose true odds of winning are now 2.0? You will need to be able to back them at 2.16 or lay them at 1.86.

On page 15 in this book there is a table that will help you to quantify the impact of commission on prices. You will then know what odds you need to better before – if all your other computations are correct – your prospective winnings start to become greater than they should be for your prospects of winning.

NEXT GOAL The only goal teams are ever trying to score is the next one. It follows that the next goal is the market from which all other score-related markets are derived. It is, therefore, one that it can be helpful to understand even if you only ever bet in-play on total goals or the final result.

In the next goal market there are always three possibilities – that the next goal will be scored by Team A, Team B or neither (in other words, that there will be no more goals).

We must, therefore, be able to answer these questions:

What are the chances of there being a next goal? And if there is a next goal, what are the chances of it being scored by Team A and what are the chances of it being scored by Team B?

In *The Definitive Guide to Betting on Sport*, I discussed ways of estimating before kick-off the proportion of goals in a match likely to be scored by each team.

Let's imagine a match in which the two teams are evenly balanced, one in which each team can be expected to score 50 per cent of the goals that are scored.

At any point during the match we can, in effect, say this – if there is another goal, there is a 50 per cent chance that it will be scored by Team A and a 50 per cent chance that it will be scored by Team B.

Let's imagine now another match, one in which the team we will call A is much stronger than the one we will call B – say, one in which Team A can be expected to score 80 per cent of the goals that are scored and Team B 20 per cent.

At any point during the 90 minutes we can, in effect, say this – if there is another goal, there is an 80 per cent chance that it

uncommon **knowledge**

**explaining
expectation**

Expect? What do we mean when we say that a team can be expected to score 80 per cent of the goals in a match?

We do not mean that today it is absolutely certain they will score 80 per cent of the goals that are scored. Obviously, the goals split can only be 80:20 if the score is 4-1, 8-2, or some other equally unlikely multiple thereof.

What we mean is that if these precise circumstances could be reproduced a great number of times – and our calculations are correct! – the team would score 80 per cent of the total number of goals scored in all those games: sometimes more, other times less, but overall 80 per cent.

Similarly, when we talk of the goals expectation in a game being 2.5 we do not mean that today there will be 2.5 goals. There can't be. Obviously, the total number of goals scored must be nought, one, two or some other whole number.

What we mean is that if these exact circumstances could be reproduced a great number of times – and, again, our calculations are correct – the total number of goals scored in all those games divided by the total number of games would be 2.5: sometimes the aggregate score would be higher, other times lower, but overall it would average 2.5.

And that is what we expect.

will be scored by Team A and a 20 per cent chance that it will be scored by Team B.

I said "in effect" because the percentages for each team can vary slightly depending on the score at that moment. When a team take the lead, the chances of them scoring the next goal can go down slightly. And vice versa.

You may have noticed this phenomenon yourself – how, within a game, the balance of play can change once the deadlock has been broken. Either the team who have gone in front sit back, trying to hold on to what they have gained – as long as they don't concede they will win. Or the team who have fallen behind now step forward, trying to grab back what they have just lost – unless they score they will lose.

Or some combination of the two.

The important point to emphasise here is that the difference this makes to the chances of each team scoring the next goal is very small – if anything, I suspect, it is more likely to be overestimated than underestimated in the betting markets.

In the Premiership and Football League in the seven seasons from 1997-98 to 2003-04, home teams scored 57.8 per cent of the goals that were scored and away teams 42.2 per cent.

What happened when the home team scored first and there was a second goal? Well, 57.5 per cent of the second goals were scored by home teams and 42.5 per cent by away teams. And what happened

WHO WILL SCORE THE NEXT GOAL?

PRE-MATCH EXPECTATION OF GOALS RATIO – 50:50

START OF MINUTE	ODDS FOR TEAM A	ODDS FOR TEAM B	NEITHER
1	2.18	2.18	11.98
6	2.20	2.20	10.90
11	2.23	2.23	9.80
16	2.26	2.26	8.76
21	2.29	2.29	7.79
26	2.34	2.34	6.91
31	2.39	2.39	6.11
36	2.46	2.46	5.39
41	2.53	2.53	4.74
46	2.65	2.65	4.05
51	2.78	2.78	3.57
56	2.95	2.95	3.11
61	3.18	3.18	2.69
66	3.51	3.51	2.32
71	4.01	4.01	2.00
76	4.81	4.81	1.71
81	6.30	6.30	1.47
86	9.95	9.95	1.25

when the away team scored first and there was a second goal? Here 58.2 per cent of the second goals were scored by home teams and 41.8 per cent by away teams.

The figures did move, but never by more than four-tenths of one per cent.

WHO WILL SCORE THE NEXT GOAL?

PRE-MATCH EXPECTATION OF GOALS RATIO – 55:45

START OF MINUTE	ODDS FOR TEAM A	ODDS FOR TEAM B	NEITHER
1	1.98	2.42	12.16
6	2.00	2.44	11.07
11	2.02	2.47	9.95
16	2.05	2.50	8.88
21	2.08	2.54	7.89
26	2.12	2.59	6.99
31	2.17	2.65	6.18
36	2.23	2.72	5.44
41	2.30	2.81	4.79
46	2.41	2.94	4.09
51	2.52	3.08	3.60
56	2.62	3.27	3.17
61	2.88	3.52	2.71
66	3.18	3.89	2.33
71	3.63	4.43	2.00
76	4.35	5.32	1.72
81	5.69	6.96	1.47
86	8.99	10.99	1.25

In the accompanying tables I have illustrated how I believe the next goal odds should be affected by changes in two variables – pre-match expectations of the proportion of goals likely to be scored by each team (which I have called the goals ratio) and how much time has elapsed.

In each table I have assumed that the pre-match goals expectation is typical for a fixture with that goals ratio. I have also assumed that the scores are still level.

Obviously, when pre-match goals expectations are higher than usual the chance, at any given moment during the match, of there being no more goals is lower than usual. And vice versa.

In addition, in all matches, the chance of there being no more goals goes down

WHO WILL SCORE THE NEXT GOAL?

PRE-MATCH EXPECTATION OF GOALS RATIO – 60:40

START OF MINUTE	ODDS FOR TEAM A	ODDS FOR TEAM B	NEITHER
1	1.81	2.72	12.37
6	1.83	2.74	11.25
11	1.85	2.77	10.10
16	1.87	2.81	9.01
21	1.90	2.86	8.01
26	1.94	2.91	7.09
31	1.98	2.98	6.25
36	2.04	3.05	5.51
41	2.10	3.15	4.84
46	2.20	3.30	4.13
51	2.30	3.45	3.63
56	2.44	3.66	3.15
61	2.63	3.95	2.72
66	2.90	4.36	2.35
71	3.31	4.97	2.01
76	3.97	5.95	1.72
81	5.19	7.79	1.47
86	8.19	12.29	1.26

slightly when the scores are no longer level – in other words, when one side or the other are winning – but the drop is never by more than about half of one per cent.

In most matches – and no matter what the score – 70 minutes or more will have to elapse before no more goals should become an odds-on shot (shorter than 2.0 in decimals).

You will see from the tables that after 70 minutes – ie. at the start of the 71st minute – in a typical match in which goals were expected to be split between the teams in a 55:45 ratio, the next goal odds should be as follows: no more goals 2.0, Team A 3.63, Team B 4.43.

In a book that does not consume every last tree still standing in the Amazon rain

WHO WILL SCORE THE NEXT GOAL?

PRE-MATCH EXPECTATION OF GOALS RATIO – 65:35

START OF MINUTE	ODDS FOR TEAM A	ODDS FOR TEAM B	NEITHER
1	1.67	3.10	12.62
6	1.69	3.13	11.47
11	1.70	3.16	10.28
16	1.73	3.21	9.17
21	1.75	3.26	8.13
26	1.79	3.32	7.19
31	1.83	3.39	6.34
36	1.87	3.48	5.58
41	1.93	3.59	4.89
46	2.02	3.76	4.17
51	2.12	3.93	3.66
56	2.24	4.17	3.18
61	2.42	4.49	2.75
66	2.67	4.96	2.36
71	3.04	5.64	2.02
76	3.64	6.76	1.73
81	4.76	8.84	1.48
86	7.51	13.95	1.26

forest, it is not possible to give tables which illustrate all goal ratios and every minute. I hope, however, that you will be able to use the tables I have provided to give yourself reasonably reliable estimates of what the next goal odds should be at most moments in most matches.

OVER/UNDER 2.5 GOALS So, now we know what the odds should be on the next goal. But how many next goals will there be?

The staple in-play market on the cumulative score is over/under 2.5 goals. If there are no, one or two goals in a game, the winners are those who bet under. If there are three or more goals, the winners are those who bet over. Obviously, this is a

WHO WILL SCORE THE NEXT GOAL?

PRE-MATCH EXPECTATION OF GOALS RATIO – 70:30

START OF MINUTE	ODDS FOR TEAM A	ODDS FOR TEAM B	NEITHER
1	1.55	3.61	12.91
6	1.56	3.64	11.72
11	1.58	3.68	10.50
16	1.60	3.73	9.35
21	1.62	3.79	8.29
26	1.65	3.86	7.32
31	1.69	3.95	6.45
36	1.73	4.05	5.66
41	1.79	4.17	4.96
46	1.87	4.37	4.23
51	1.96	4.57	3.70
56	2.07	4.84	3.21
61	2.24	5.22	2.77
66	2.46	5.75	2.38
71	2.81	6.55	2.04
76	3.36	7.84	1.74
81	4.39	10.24	1.48
86	6.92	16.14	1.26

market that can be traded unless or until a third goal is scored.

To be able to estimate the chances of a game finishing with fewer or more than 2.5 goals, we need to know two things. We need to know how many goals have been scored so far. And we need to know how many goals are likely to be scored in whatever time remains.

The higher the pre-match goals expectation was, the greater the number of goals that are likely to be scored during however many minutes are still to be played.

In *The Definitive Guide to Betting on Sport* I described ways of estimating the pre-match goals expectation.

To recap, briefly: the total number of goals likely to be scored in a match is

WHO WILL SCORE THE NEXT GOAL?

PRE-MATCH EXPECTATION OF GOALS RATIO – 75:25

START OF MINUTE	ODDS FOR TEAM A	ODDS FOR TEAM B	NEITHER
1	1.44	4.33	13.26
6	1.45	4.36	12.02
11	1.47	4.41	10.76
16	1.49	4.47	9.57
21	1.51	4.54	8.47
26	1.54	4.62	7.47
31	1.57	4.72	6.57
36	1.61	4.84	5.76
41	1.66	4.99	5.04
46	1.74	5.22	4.29
51	1.82	5.45	3.75
56	1.93	5.78	3.25
61	2.07	6.22	2.80
66	2.29	6.86	2.40
71	2.60	7.80	2.05
76	3.11	9.33	1.75
81	4.06	12.19	1.49
86	6.40	19.19	1.26

influenced by two factors above all others – the relative abilities of the teams and the goals histories of the teams. The first is three times as important as the second.

Let's consider a practical example: a game at a neutral venue between two mid-table teams from the same division – in other words, a game in which each team can be expected to score 50 per cent of the goals that are scored. The typical goals expectation in such a game would be around 2.5.

Let's suppose, though, that one team's games have been averaging 2.9 goals and the other's 3.1. In other words, one team's games have been producing 1.16 times as many goals as normal for a mid-table outfit $(2.9 \div 2.5 = 1.16)$ and the other team's

WHO WILL SCORE THE NEXT GOAL?

PRE-MATCH EXPECTATION OF GOALS RATIO – 80:20

START OF MINUTE	ODDS FOR TEAM A	ODDS FOR TEAM B	NEITHER
1	1.35	5.39	13.70
6	1.36	5.44	12.41
11	1.37	5.50	11.09
16	1.39	5.57	9.85
21	1.41	5.65	8.70
26	1.44	5.75	7.66
31	1.47	5.87	6.73
36	1.51	6.02	5.89
41	1.55	6.21	5.15
46	1.62	6.48	4.37
51	1.69	6.78	3.82
56	1.79	7.18	3.30
61	1.93	7.73	2.83
66	2.13	8.50	2.43
71	2.42	9.67	2.07
76	2.89	11.56	1.76
81	3.77	15.07	1.50
86	5.93	23.72	1.27

games have been producing 1.24 times as many ($3.1 \prod 2.5 = 1.24$).

You could get a perfectly reliable estimate of what the goals expectation should be for this match by using a reasonably simple calculation: $(2.5 \times 0.75) + (2.5 \times 1.16 \times 1.24 \times 0.25) = 2.8$. We are giving three times as much weight to the typical goals expectation for a fixture with this goals ratio expectation as we are to the goals histories of the teams.

The theory is actually a bit more complicated than I have intimated here. In practice, though, you don't need to worry about those complications.

The typical goals expectation never varies very much, no matter what the goals ratio expectation – the more goals the favourites are expected to score, the fewer the outsiders are expected to score.

In the tables below, I have illustrated how I believe the chances of a match finishing with fewer or more than 2.5 goals varies at different times according to the number of goals that have been scored so far and the pre-match goals expectation.

In the real world, you will rarely encounter a game with a goals expectation much lower than 2.2 or higher than 3.2. In theory, the chances of over/under 2.5 goals are influenced by which team scores the first goal and whether or not the second goal is an equaliser. In practice, you can safely ignore these influences.

HOW MANY GOALS WILL THERE BE?

PRE-MATCH EXPECTATION: 2.2

	SO FAR: 0 ODDS FOR:		SO FAR: 1 ODDS FOR:		SO FAR: 2 ODDS FOR:	
START OF MINUTE	UNDER 2.5	OVER 2.5	UNDER 2.5	OVER 2.5	UNDER 2.5	OVER 2.5
1	1.60	2.66	—	—	—	—
6	1.55	2.83	2.64	1.61	7.95	1.14
11	1.49	3.05	2.48	1.68	7.25	1.16
16	1.43	3.33	2.32	1.76	6.57	1.18
21	1.37	3.67	2.17	1.86	5.94	1.20
26	1.32	4.10	2.02	1.98	5.35	1.23
31	1.27	4.65	1.89	2.12	4.81	1.26
36	1.23	5.35	1.77	2.31	4.31	1.30
41	1.19	6.28	1.65	2.54	3.86	1.35
46	1.15	7.86	1.53	2.90	3.37	1.42
51	1.12	9.70	1.44	3.30	3.01	1.50
56	1.09	12.60	1.35	3.88	2.67	1.60
61	1.06	17.34	1.27	4.75	2.36	1.74
66	1.04	25.73	1.20	6.12	2.07	1.93
71	1.02	42.35	1.13	8.52	1.82	2.22
76	1.01	81.58	1.08	13.37	1.59	2.68
81	1.00	205.11	1.04	26.21	1.39	3.55
86	1.00	895.32	1.01	90.78	1.21	5.66

HOW MANY GOALS WILL THERE BE?

PRE-MATCH EXPECTATION: 2.4

START OF MINUTE	SO FAR: 0 ODDS FOR:		SO FAR: 1 ODDS FOR:		SO FAR: 2 ODDS FOR:	
	UNDER 2.5	OVER 2.5	UNDER 2.5	OVER 2.5	UNDER 2.5	OVER 2.5
1	1.75	2.34	—	—	—	—
6	1.68	2.47	3.01	1.50	9.57	1.12
11	1.60	2.65	2.80	1.55	8.66	1.13
16	1.53	2.88	2.60	1.62	7.78	1.15
21	1.46	3.16	2.41	1.71	6.97	1.17
26	1.40	3.51	2.23	1.81	6.22	1.19
31	1.34	3.95	2.07	1.94	5.53	1.22
36	1.28	4.52	1.92	2.09	4.91	1.26
41	1.23	5.28	1.78	2.29	4.35	1.30
46	1.18	6.55	1.63	2.60	3.76	1.36
51	1.14	8.02	1.52	2.94	3.33	1.43
56	1.11	10.35	1.41	3.43	2.92	1.52
61	1.08	14.14	1.32	4.17	2.55	1.65
66	1.05	20.81	1.23	5.33	2.22	1.82
71	1.03	33.98	1.16	7.35	1.92	2.08
76	1.02	64.92	1.10	11.41	1.66	2.51
81	1.01	161.97	1.05	21.95	1.44	3.30
86	1.00	703.30	1.01	72.41	1.24	5.23

In my experience, betting markets can sometimes read too much into teams' goals histories. We have learnt that they are important, but not that important. It is also possible that betting markets will some-times read too much into the number of goals that have been scored so far – almost certainly, if they do move in the wrong direction it will be to over-react rather than under-react.

In an article in the *Racing Post* I have shown that when a goal is scored in the first ten minutes of a match the number of goals that are likely to be scored in the remaining 80 minutes is, to all intents and purposes,

HOW MANY GOALS WILL THERE BE?

PRE-MATCH EXPECTATION: 2.6

	SO FAR: 0 ODDS FOR:		SO FAR: 1 ODDS FOR:		SO FAR: 2 ODDS FOR:	
START OF MINUTE	UNDER 2.5	OVER 2.5	UNDER 2.5	OVER 2.5	UNDER 2.5	OVER 2.5
1	1.92	2.09	—	—	—	—
6	1.83	2.20	3.45	1.41	11.53	1.09
11	1.74	2.35	3.18	1.46	10.34	1.11
16	1.65	2.54	2.93	1.52	9.22	1.12
21	1.56	2.77	2.69	1.59	8.18	1.14
26	1.49	3.06	2.47	1.68	7.23	1.16
31	1.41	3.43	2.27	1.79	6.37	1.19
36	1.34	3.90	2.09	1.92	5.60	1.22
41	1.28	4.52	1.92	2.09	4.91	1.26
46	1.22	5.57	1.74	2.36	4.19	1.31
51	1.17	6.78	1.61	2.65	3.68	1.37
56	1.13	8.68	1.48	3.08	3.19	1.46
61	1.09	11.77	1.37	3.72	2.75	1.57
66	1.06	17.18	1.27	4.72	2.37	1.73
71	1.04	27.83	1.18	6.45	2.03	1.97
76	1.02	52.74	1.11	9.89	1.73	2.36
81	1.01	130.53	1.06	18.72	1.48	3.09
86	1.00	563.40	1.02	59.42	1.26	4.87

exactly what we would have anticipated from the pre-match goals expectation.

In other words, when there are a flurry of early goals it does not follow that scoring will continue at the same high rate – or even at a higher rate at all. Yet there may sometimes be players in the betting markets who mistakenly think that it will.

RESULT So, now we know the likelihood of each team scoring the next goal, if there is one. And how many next goals there are likely to be, if there are any at all. We can begin to answer the question that is most meaningful to most people in most matches: who will win, if anyone does?

HOW MANY GOALS WILL THERE BE?

PRE-MATCH EXPECTATION: 2.8

START OF MINUTE	SO FAR: 0 ODDS FOR:		SO FAR: 1 ODDS FOR:		SO FAR: 2 ODDS FOR:	
	UNDER 2.5	OVER 2.5	UNDER 2.5	OVER 2.5	UNDER 2.5	OVER 2.5
1	2.12	1.89	—	—	—	—
6	2.01	1.99	3.95	1.34	13.88	1.08
11	1.89	2.12	3.62	1.38	12.35	1.09
16	1.78	2.28	3.31	1.43	10.91	1.10
21	1.68	2.47	3.02	1.50	9.59	1.12
26	1.58	2.71	2.75	1.57	8.40	1.14
31	1.49	3.02	2.50	1.67	7.33	1.16
36	1.41	3.42	2.27	1.78	6.39	1.19
41	1.34	3.94	2.07	1.93	5.55	1.22
46	1.26	4.81	1.86	2.17	4.67	1.27
51	1.21	5.83	1.70	2.42	4.06	1.33
56	1.16	7.41	1.56	2.80	3.48	1.40
61	1.11	9.97	1.43	3.35	2.97	1.51
66	1.07	14.44	1.31	4.22	2.53	1.65
71	1.05	23.20	1.21	5.72	2.14	1.88
76	1.02	43.60	1.13	8.69	1.81	2.24
81	1.01	107.04	1.07	16.22	1.52	2.91
86	1.00	458.99	1.02	49.84	1.28	4.56

It may be helpful, though, to pause here for a moment and wring our hands a little bit more thoroughly over a subject that we have only touched on before.

Should our expectations of what will happen in the rest of a match be based on what we thought about the teams before the match began or how well they have played so far?

In almost everything I have said so far there is an implicit assumption that the correct answer is: what we thought about the teams before the match began. And although I cannot prove this conclusively, I am convinced it is so.

HOW MANY GOALS WILL THERE BE?

PRE-MATCH EXPECTATION: 3.0

START OF	SO FAR: 0 ODDS FOR:		SO FAR: 1 ODDS FOR:		SO FAR: 2 ODDS FOR:	
	UNDER	OVER	UNDER	OVER	UNDER	OVER
1	2.35	1.74	—	—	—	—
6	2.21	1.83	4.55	1.28	16.72	1.06
11	2.07	1.93	4.14	1.32	14.75	1.07
16	1.94	2.07	3.75	1.36	12.91	1.08
21	1.81	2.23	3.38	1.42	11.25	1.10
26	1.69	2.44	3.05	1.49	9.76	1.11
31	1.59	2.70	2.75	1.57	8.44	1.13
36	1.49	3.04	2.49	1.67	7.28	1.16
41	1.40	3.49	2.24	1.80	6.26	1.19
46	1.31	4.23	1.99	2.01	5.21	1.24
51	1.25	5.08	1.81	2.24	4.48	1.29
56	1.18	6.42	1.64	2.57	3.80	1.36
61	1.13	8.57	1.49	3.06	3.21	1.45
66	1.09	12.32	1.35	3.82	2.70	1.59
71	1.05	19.63	1.24	5.14	2.26	1.79
76	1.03	36.59	1.15	7.73	1.89	2.13
81	1.01	89.10	1.08	14.23	1.57	2.75
86	1.00	379.43	1.02	42.55	1.30	4.30

Certainly, every odds-maker and market-maker I have ever spoken to at a fixed-odds or spread bookmaker who bets in-running has given me the same response. And as nearly all of them make a profit from their in-play activities season after season, this seems a pretty big clue.

I look at it like this. Our assessments of the teams before the match began are likely to have been based on rather more evidence than the 30, 40, 50 minutes or whatever of play that we have witnessed so far today – and, therefore, they are likely to be more reliable. I will give you an example of what I mean.

I thought PSV Eindhoven were being dismissed too lightly in some betting

HOW MANY GOALS WILL THERE BE?

PRE-MATCH EXPECTATION: 3.2

START OF MINUTE	SO FAR: 0 ODDS FOR:		SO FAR: 1 ODDS FOR:		SO FAR: 2 ODDS FOR:	
	UNDER 2.5	OVER 2.5	UNDER 2.5	OVER 2.5	UNDER 2.5	OVER 2.5
1	2.61	1.62	—	—	—	—
6	2.44	1.69	5.24	1.24	20.13	1.05
11	2.27	1.79	4.73	1.27	17.61	1.06
16	2.11	1.90	4.25	1.31	15.29	1.07
21	1.96	2.04	3.81	1.36	13.20	1.08
26	1.82	2.22	3.40	1.42	11.34	1.10
31	1.69	2.45	3.04	1.49	9.71	1.11
36	1.57	2.74	2.72	1.58	8.29	1.14
41	1.47	3.12	2.43	1.70	7.06	1.16
46	1.36	3.76	2.13	1.88	5.81	1.21
51	1.29	4.49	1.92	2.08	4.94	1.25
56	1.22	5.63	1.73	2.38	4.15	1.32
61	1.15	7.47	1.55	2.81	3.47	1.41
66	1.10	10.65	1.40	3.49	2.88	1.53
71	1.06	16.83	1.27	4.66	2.38	1.72
76	1.03	31.11	1.17	6.94	1.97	2.03
81	1.01	75.15	1.09	12.63	1.62	2.62
86	1.00	317.69	1.03	36.85	1.33	4.06

markets before their 2005 Champions League semi-final against Milan. Anyone who watched the two matches would surely agree that on the balance of play over 180 minutes Guus Hiddink's Dutch champions were unlucky to lose.

Yet, equally, anyone who watched the first ten minutes of the opener at the San Siro, and formed an opinion based solely on what they had just witnessed, could only have reached one conclusion – and that was that Milan would slaughter PSV by an aggregate score that could become embarrassing, even humiliating. The next 170 minutes, though, were nothing like the first ten.

On occasions, however, teams will play

throughout a contest in a way that is completely different from what it was reasonable to have predicted of them beforehand. In a 2005 Champions League second-leg tie at Highbury, visitors Bayern Munich played much differently and a lot better than most people – myself included – had expected, while hosts Arsenal played much differently and a lot worse. The exchange odds expressed this gradually dawning realisation, and it was right for them to do so.

The best policy is probably to assume that nearly always a team will play for the rest of the match as we had imagined they

WHO WILL WIN?

PRE-MATCH ODDS: 2.79 TEAM A, 3.53 DRAW, 2.79 TEAM B

STATE OF PLAY:

START OF MINUTE	A+2 ODDS FOR:				A+1 ODDS FOR:		
	A	X	B		A	X	B
6	1.19	8.93	20.23		1.59	4.54	6.65
11	1.18	9.13	21.78		1.58	4.50	6.91
16	1.18	9.37	23.69		1.57	4.46	7.22
21	1.17	9.67	26.05		1.56	4.43	7.60
26	1.16	10.04	28.98		1.54	4.40	8.04
31	1.14	10.49	32.67		1.53	4.38	8.58
36	1.13	11.05	37.41		1.51	4.36	9.23
41	1.12	11.76	43.61		1.49	4.36	10.04
46	1.11	12.87	53.96		1.46	4.37	11.31
51	1.09	14.08	65.90		1.44	4.41	12.67
56	1.08	15.82	84.54		1.41	4.49	14.62
61	1.07	18.36	114.55		1.38	4.62	17.46
66	1.05	22.26	166.75		1.34	4.84	21.85
71	1.04	28.75	268.49		1.29	5.21	29.18
76	1.03	40.96	504.41		1.24	5.85	43.11
81	1.02	69.17	1235.67		1.18	7.13	75.88
86	1.01	176.44	5322.66		1.11	10.37	194.19

would play throughout the match, but accept – and be ever alert to the possibility – that this will not always be so.

In the tables starting below I have shown how I believe the odds on each of the three possible results – a win for Team A, a draw or a win for Team B – should change during a game according to the score at the time and how long is left to be played.

You will see that there are five different tables, each of which relates to a different set of pre-match odds. The first one, for example, is appropriate for a match in which each team is considered before kick-off to be as likely to win as the other, a

STATE OF PLAY:

	0 ODDS FOR:			B+1 ODDS FOR:			B+2 ODDS FOR:	
A	X	B	A	X	B	A	X	B
2.82	3.46	2.82	6.65	4.54	1.59	20.23	8.93	1.19
2.85	3.37	2.85	6.91	4.50	1.58	21.78	9.13	1.18
2.88	3.27	2.88	7.22	4.46	1.57	23.69	9.37	1.18
2.92	3.17	2.92	7.60	4.43	1.56	26.05	9.67	1.17
2.97	3.07	2.97	8.04	4.40	1.54	28.98	10.04	1.16
3.03	2.95	3.03	8.58	4.38	1.53	32.67	10.49	1.14
3.09	2.83	3.09	9.23	4.36	1.51	37.41	11.05	1.13
3.17	2.71	3.17	10.04	4.36	1.49	43.61	11.76	1.12
3.30	2.55	3.30	11.31	4.37	1.46	53.96	12.87	1.11
3.42	2.41	3.42	12.67	4.41	1.44	65.90	14.08	1.09
3.59	2.26	3.59	14.62	4.49	1.41	84.54	15.82	1.08
3.82	2.10	3.82	17.46	4.62	1.38	114.55	18.36	1.07
4.15	1.93	4.15	21.85	4.84	1.34	166.75	22.26	1.05
4.64	1.76	4.64	29.18	5.21	1.29	268.49	28.75	1.04
5.43	1.58	5.43	43.11	5.85	1.24	504.41	40.96	1.03
6.92	1.41	6.92	75.88	7.13	1.18	1235.67	69.17	1.02
10.58	1.23	10.58	194.19	10.37	1.11	5322.66	176.44	1.01

WHO WILL WIN?

PRE-MATCH ODDS: 2.25 TEAM A, 3.61 DRAW, 3.59 TEAM B
STATE OF PLAY:

START OF MINUTE	A+2 ODDS FOR:			A+1 ODDS FOR:		
	A	X	B	A	X	B
6	1.13	11.95	33.10	1.41	5.31	9.59
11	1.12	12.21	35.53	1.41	5.26	9.93
16	1.12	12.53	38.54	1.41	5.21	10.34
21	1.11	12.91	42.25	1.40	5.17	10.83
26	1.11	13.39	46.87	1.39	5.13	11.41
31	1.10	13.98	52.69	1.39	5.09	12.12
36	1.09	14.71	60.15	1.38	5.07	13.00
41	1.09	15.63	69.92	1.37	5.06	14.08
46	1.08	17.09	86.20	1.35	5.07	15.77
51	1.07	18.66	104.98	1.34	5.11	17.59
56	1.06	20.95	134.25	1.32	5.19	20.21
61	1.05	24.28	181.28	1.30	5.34	24.04
66	1.04	29.41	262.86	1.27	5.58	29.92
71	1.03	37.93	421.39	1.24	6.00	39.75
76	1.02	53.97	787.65	1.20	6.74	58.41
81	1.01	91.02	1918.13	1.15	8.20	102.19
86	1.00	229.98	8205.06	1.10	11.89	259.78

match in which the correct odds at the first whistle would be 2.79 for a win by Team A, 3.53 for a draw and 2.79 for a win by Team B.

The tables are then sub-divided into five columns, each of which relates to a different state of play. If the scores are still level, use the one headed 0. If Team A are leading by one goal, use the one headed A+1. If Team B are leading by one goal, use the one headed B+1. And so on.

Each row gives the odds for A, X and B – a win for Team A, a draw and a win for Team B – at the start of every five minute period within the game.

So, for example, if Team A are leading

STATE OF PLAY:

O			B+1			B+2		
ODDS FOR:			ODDS FOR:			ODDS FOR:		
A	X	B	A	X	B	A	X	B
2.28	3.53	3.61	4.79	4.06	1.84	12.89	6.98	1.28
2.31	3.44	3.63	4.99	4.02	1.82	13.89	7.13	1.27
2.34	3.34	3.66	5.23	3.98	1.79	15.13	7.32	1.25
2.38	3.23	3.69	5.51	3.95	1.77	16.65	7.54	1.24
2.43	3.12	3.74	5.85	3.92	1.74	18.55	7.82	1.22
2.48	3.00	3.79	6.25	3.89	1.72	20.94	8.16	1.21
2.55	2.88	3.85	6.74	3.87	1.69	24.00	8.59	1.19
2.62	2.74	3.93	7.36	3.86	1.65	28.01	9.12	1.17
2.74	2.58	4.06	8.31	3.87	1.61	34.70	9.97	1.15
2.85	2.44	4.18	9.33	3.90	1.57	42.43	10.89	1.13
3.00	2.28	4.37	10.79	3.96	1.53	54.50	12.22	1.11
3.21	2.12	4.62	12.93	4.07	1.48	73.96	14.17	1.09
3.50	1.95	4.98	16.22	4.26	1.42	107.85	17.15	1.07
3.94	1.77	5.53	21.73	4.58	1.36	174.03	22.12	1.05
4.64	1.59	6.43	32.20	5.14	1.29	327.81	31.47	1.04
5.94	1.41	8.13	56.89	6.26	1.22	805.65	53.07	1.02
9.13	1.24	12.32	146.18	9.09	1.13	3484.29	136.03	1.01

by one goal at the start of the 21st minute – and pre-match assessments were accurate – the correct odds would now be 1.56 for a victory by Team A, 4.43 for a draw and 7.60 for a victory by Team B.

In a book that is small enough to fit through your front door, there is not room to illustrate more than a tiny number of the almost limitless possible combinations of pre-match odds. I have chosen four more, in which Team A become progressively stronger than Team B and the correct odds before kick-off for a victory by Team A are 2.25, 1.80, 1.50 and 1.33.

In each example, the prospects before kick-off for a victory by Team A increase

WHO WILL WIN?

PRE-MATCH ODDS: 1.80 TEAM A, 3.93 DRAW, 5.27 TEAM B
STATE OF PLAY:

START OF MINUTE	A+2 ODDS FOR: A	X	B	A+1 ODDS FOR: A	X	B
6	1.07	18.88	69.07	1.26	6.92	16.61
11	1.07	19.22	73.79	1.26	6.83	17.09
16	1.07	19.65	79.63	1.26	6.74	17.68
21	1.07	20.19	86.86	1.26	6.66	18.39
26	1.06	20.86	95.86	1.26	6.58	19.25
31	1.06	21.70	107.23	1.25	6.51	20.30
36	1.06	22.76	121.83	1.25	6.45	21.61
41	1.05	24.10	140.94	1.25	6.41	23.26
46	1.05	26.25	172.81	1.24	6.40	25.84
51	1.04	28.58	209.52	1.24	6.43	28.64
56	1.04	31.98	266.65	1.23	6.50	32.68
61	1.03	36.96	358.25	1.21	6.66	38.58
66	1.03	44.63	516.57	1.20	6.94	47.68
71	1.02	57.40	822.85	1.18	7.43	62.86
76	1.01	81.44	1526.67	1.15	8.32	91.60
81	1.01	137.00	3685.65	1.12	10.09	158.87
86	1.00	342.33	15605.43	1.08	14.59	400.04

by roughly ten per cent – from 36 per cent to 44 to 56 to 67 and then 75.

I should add that the decimal odds shown here have been rounded to the nearest 0.01. So when the second table says that if a team whose odds at kick-off were 2.25 are leading by two goals at the start of the 86th minute their odds should now be 1.00, it does not mean that they are certain to win – obviously, they can't be – but that they are almost certain to win, and that their odds are now closer to 1.00 than 1.01.

In each example I have assumed a typical pre-match goals expectation.

I hope that you will be able to use these tables to give yourself a reasonable impres-

				STATE OF PLAY:				
	O ODDS FOR:			*B+1* ODDS FOR:			*B+2* ODDS FOR:	
A	*X*	*B*	*A*	*X*	*B*	*A*	*X*	*B*
1.82	3.83	5.26	3.39	3.73	2.29	7.93	5.49	1.45
1.85	3.71	5.26	3.53	3.68	2.25	8.54	5.59	1.42
1.88	3.59	5.26	3.70	3.63	2.20	9.31	5.71	1.39
1.92	3.45	5.27	3.90	3.59	2.15	10.25	5.87	1.37
1.96	3.32	5.28	4.15	3.54	2.10	11.42	6.06	1.34
2.01	3.17	5.31	4.44	3.50	2.04	12.89	6.30	1.31
2.07	3.03	5.36	4.80	3.47	1.99	14.79	6.61	1.28
2.14	2.87	5.42	5.24	3.45	1.93	17.26	7.00	1.25
2.24	2.68	5.53	5.93	3.44	1.85	21.39	7.62	1.22
2.34	2.53	5.66	6.67	3.45	1.78	26.17	8.29	1.19
2.48	2.35	5.85	7.74	3.49	1.71	33.64	9.27	1.16
2.66	2.17	6.12	9.29	3.58	1.63	45.70	10.71	1.13
2.91	1.99	6.54	11.68	3.73	1.55	66.73	12.93	1.10
3.29	1.80	7.18	15.69	3.99	1.46	107.87	16.63	1.07
3.89	1.61	8.26	23.33	4.47	1.36	203.67	23.58	1.05
5.01	1.42	10.31	41.37	5.43	1.26	502.06	39.66	1.03
7.75	1.24	15.46	106.73	7.86	1.16	2179.94	102.31	1.01

sion of what the odds should be on each of the three possible results at many moments in many matches, no matter what the score or how long is left to be played.

CORNERS The first thing to understand about total corners is that the market is not related to total goals, despite what many bettors seem to think.

You may have heard people say that in a game that is expected to be cagey and low-scoring there will not be many corners – and, conversely, that in a game where both teams are expected to be gung-ho and free-scoring there will be lots of corners.

As a general rule, it isn't true.

WHO WILL WIN?

PRE-MATCH ODDS: 1.50 TEAM A, 4.59 DRAW, 8.69 TEAM B
STATE OF PLAY:

START OF MINUTE	A+2 ODDS FOR: A	X	B	A+1 ODDS FOR: A	X	B
6	1.04	34.78	178.12	1.15	10.02	33.64
11	1.04	35.20	189.00	1.15	9.82	34.32
16	1.03	35.77	202.55	1.15	9.63	35.17
21	1.03	36.52	219.40	1.15	9.43	36.25
26	1.03	37.50	240.49	1.16	9.25	37.60
31	1.03	38.78	267.21	1.16	9.09	39.30
36	1.03	40.43	301.61	1.16	8.94	41.45
41	1.03	42.57	346.77	1.16	8.83	44.21
46	1.02	46.05	422.16	1.16	8.74	48.62
51	1.02	49.89	509.04	1.15	8.71	53.44
56	1.02	55.51	644.11	1.15	8.76	60.45
61	1.02	63.82	860.15	1.14	8.91	70.76
66	1.01	76.69	1232.13	1.14	9.23	86.65
71	1.01	98.19	1947.86	1.12	9.82	113.18
76	1.01	138.71	3581.51	1.11	10.93	163.32
81	1.00	232.42	8553.19	1.09	13.19	280.24
86	1.00	575.09	35751.26	1.06	19.01	697.51

The average number of corners in Premiership games in the eight seasons between 1997-98 and 2004-05 was 11.1. In games where there were no goals, the average number of corners was 11.1. In games where there was one goal, the average number of corners was 11.2. In games where there were two goals, the average number of corners was 11.1. In games where there were three goals, the average number of corners was 11.2. In games where there were four or more goals, the average number of corners was 10.9.

The greater the proportion of goals in a game that a team scores, the greater the

	O ODDS FOR:			B+1 ODDS FOR:			B+2 ODDS FOR:	
A	X	B	A	X	B	A	X	B
1.52	4.44	8.60	2.51	3.64	3.06	5.19	4.59	1.70
1.54	4.27	8.51	2.62	3.57	2.96	5.58	4.64	1.65
1.57	4.08	8.42	2.75	3.49	2.86	6.07	4.72	1.60
1.60	3.90	8.35	2.90	3.42	2.76	6.68	4.81	1.56
1.64	3.71	8.28	3.08	3.36	2.66	7.43	4.94	1.51
1.68	3.51	8.23	3.29	3.29	2.55	8.38	5.11	1.46
1.73	3.32	8.20	3.56	3.24	2.44	9.60	5.32	1.41
1.79	3.12	8.21	3.89	3.20	2.33	11.20	5.60	1.37
1.88	2.88	8.25	4.40	3.16	2.19	13.87	6.06	1.31
1.97	2.68	8.35	4.95	3.15	2.08	16.95	6.56	1.27
2.09	2.48	8.52	5.74	3.17	1.96	21.78	7.29	1.22
2.25	2.26	8.81	6.90	3.22	1.84	29.58	8.38	1.18
2.47	2.05	9.28	8.69	3.33	1.71	43.20	10.06	1.14
2.80	1.84	10.05	11.69	3.55	1.58	69.86	12.88	1.10
3.32	1.64	11.40	17.41	3.95	1.45	132.05	18.18	1.07
4.30	1.44	14.03	30.94	4.78	1.32	326.13	30.46	1.04
6.68	1.25	20.69	80.06	6.89	1.19	1420.02	79.09	1.01

STATE OF PLAY:

proportion of corners they are likely to gain. But, as we have seen, rises and falls in the total number of goals scored do not produce corresponding rises and falls in the total number of corners gained.

And it is the total number of corners gained that interests us here.

On betting exchanges, you can usually either offer or accept odds on three possibilities – nine corners or fewer, between ten and 12, or 13 and more.

The first thing we have got to be able to do here is estimate the corners expectation for the match – if these two teams played over and over again, under precisely these

WHO WILL WIN?

PRE-MATCH ODDS: 1.33 TEAM A, 5.52 DRAW, 14.61 TEAM B
STATE OF PLAY:

START OF MINUTE	A+2 ODDS FOR:			A+1 ODDS FOR:		
	A	X	B	A	X	B
6	1.02	66.45	474.74	1.09	14.94	69.43
11	1.02	66.79	500.28	1.09	14.53	70.20
16	1.02	67.40	532.41	1.09	14.11	71.29
21	1.02	68.33	572.66	1.10	13.71	72.80
26	1.02	69.67	623.40	1.10	13.33	74.82
31	1.02	71.53	688.06	1.10	12.98	77.50
36	1.02	74.06	771.67	1.10	12.67	81.03
41	1.01	77.47	881.86	1.10	12.40	85.67
46	1.01	83.15	1066.32	1.10	12.15	93.28
51	1.01	89.54	1279.23	1.10	12.02	101.73
56	1.01	99.04	1610.21	1.10	11.99	114.16
61	1.01	113.19	2138.82	1.10	12.10	132.54
66	1.01	135.25	3045.85	1.09	12.44	160.97
71	1.01	172.26	4781.91	1.09	13.16	208.45
76	1.00	242.17	8717.03	1.08	14.56	297.98
81	1.00	403.99	20594.63	1.06	17.48	506.06
86	1.00·	993.86	84962.37	1.04	25.07	1245.41

conditions, what is the average number of corners that would be taken?

Once we have estimated the corners expectation, we can estimate the chances of today's total being any given number from nought upwards.

The corners histories of teams have more influence on the total number of corners likely to be awarded than the goals histories of teams have on the total number of goals likely to be scored. But, even so, the typical corners total for a match in that competition still has one and a half times as much influence as the individual corners histories of the two participating teams.

Let's imagine a fixture in a competition

STATE OF PLAY:								
0			B+1			B+2		
ODDS FOR:			ODDS FOR:			ODDS FOR:		
A	X	B	A	X	B	A	X	B
1.35	5.29	14.34	2.05	3.74	4.08	3.85	4.16	2.00
1.37	5.03	14.04	2.14	3.63	3.90	4.14	4.18	1.93
1.39	4.76	13.75	2.24	3.53	3.72	4.50	4.22	1.85
1.42	4.50	13.47	2.35	3.42	3.53	4.93	4.27	1.78
1.45	4.23	13.22	2.50	3.33	3.35	5.48	4.36	1.70
1.49	3.96	12.99	2.67	3.24	3.16	6.17	4.47	1.63
1.54	3.69	12.79	2.88	3.16	2.98	7.05	4.63	1.56
1.59	3.43	12.64	3.14	3.09	2.79	8.20	4.84	1.49
1.67	3.12	12.54	3.55	3.02	2.58	10.14	5.19	1.41
1.74	2.88	12.53	3.99	2.99	2.41	12.37	5.58	1.35
1.85	2.63	12.63	4.63	2.98	2.23	15.87	6.17	1.29
1.99	2.38	12.88	5.56	3.01	2.05	21.52	7.05	1.23
2.19	2.13	13.39	7.00	3.09	1.87	31.40	8.41	1.18
2.49	1.89	14.30	9.41	3.27	1.70	50.75	10.71	1.13
2.96	1.67	15.97	14.03	3.63	1.53	95.90	15.04	1.08
3.83	1.45	19.36	24.95	4.36	1.37	236.93	25.57	1.05
5.98	1.25	28.09	64.68	6.28	1.21	1032.86	65.45	1.02

where the average total for corners is 11.5. We will call the competing teams, as we usually do, A and B. Let's suppose that Team A's games have been averaging 10.5 corners while Team B's games have been averaging 10.2. That is to say, Team A's games have been producing only 0.91 times as many corners as normal for a team in that competition and Team B's games just 0.89 times as many.

We can get a perfectly serviceable estimate of the corners expectation for today's meeting by using this calculation: (11.5 x 0.6) + (11.5 x 0.91 x 0.89 x 0.4) = 10.6. We are giving one and a half times as much weight to the typical corners total for a match in that competition as we are to the individual corners histories of the two participating teams (we are multiplying the former by 0.6 and the latter by 0.4).

In my opinion, bettors may sometimes pay too much attention to the corners histories of teams in the total corners market, just as they may sometimes pay too much attention to the goals histories of teams in the total goals market. Put it this way – if the odds are ever wrong in a game between two teams whose previous engagements have produced an exceptionally large number of flag-kicks, it will almost certainly be because they overestimate the likelihood of another sky-high haul. And vice versa.

In the table below I have given what I believe to be the correct odds at kick-off for 0-9 corners, 10-12 and 13+ in fixtures with a variety of pre-match corners expectations.

SPREADFAIR It's not only fixed-odds betting that is available on exchanges. You can now play the spreads, too.

Spreadfair was launched in June 2004 by Cantor Sport.

The conventional spread betting firms insist that it has not affected their turnover.

And when Sporting and IG reduced the width of their spreads on a number of major football markets during the 2004-05 season, they protested vehemently that it was not because of competition from Spreadfair – even before anyone had asked them.

Yet whether by accident or design, these

HOW MANY CORNERS WILL THERE BE?

PRE-MATCH EXPECTATION

ACTUAL TOTAL	9.00	9.20	9.40	9.60	9.80	10.00	10.20	10.40	10.60	10.80	11.00
0 TO 9	1.74	1.81	1.90	1.99	2.08	2.19	2.30	2.42	2.55	2.69	2.84
10 TO 12	3.66	3.55	3.46	3.39	3.33	3.28	3.24	3.22	3.20	3.20	3.20
13 PLUS	6.61	5.98	5.44	4.97	4.57	4.21	3.90	3.63	3.39	3.17	2.98

reduced-width spreads are comparable to those that are often available on Spreadfair, after allowance for commission. On Spreadfair, as on the fixed-odds betting exchanges, you have to pay up to five per cent of your profit from winning bets in commission.

Because the consensus in the Spreadfair market is not always, if ever, identical to that of the Sporting, IG or Spreadex market-makers, there are still times when the best-value trades are obtainable on Spreadfair. Sometimes you are better off with Spreadfair, sometimes not. You have to continually monitor all outlets.

It is harder to quantify the impact of commission on a spread trade than it is on a fixed-odds bet. In an article in the *Racing Post*, I suggested that paying five per cent commission on a spread supremacy trade was equivalent to accepting a price that was worse than the screen price by fewer than seven-hundredths of a goal (0.07), and that for total corners the difference was smaller than two-tenths of one corner (0.2).

I don't say that these figure are unquestionably correct − only that nobody complained they were incorrect, and that my private, completely unofficial soundings at Cantor Sport gave me the impression that Spreadfair's operators thought they were about right.

In the tables starting alongside I have shown how I believe supremacy and total goals expectations − supremacy and total goals are the staple, in-play spread

11.20	11.40	11.60	11.80	12.00	12.20	12.40	12.60	12.80	13.00
3.01	3.18	3.37	3.58	3.80	4.05	4.31	4.59	4.90	5.23
3.21	3.23	3.26	3.30	3.34	3.39	3.45	3.52	3.60	3.68
2.81	2.66	2.52	2.40	2.29	2.18	2.09	2.01	1.93	1.86

markets – decay during the 90 minutes of a match.

After an hour – ie. at the start of the 61st minute – of a match in which the correct supremacy expectation at kick-off was 0.5 favourites/outsiders, the supremacy expectation for the remaining half-hour would be 0.2 favourites/outsiders.

If the scores were still level, the appropriate price in the supremacy spread market would be 0.2 favourites/outsiders. If the favourites were leading by one goal, it would be 1.2 favourites/outsiders. If the outsiders were leading by one goal, it would be 0.8 outsiders/favourites. And so on.

The same principle applies to the goals expectation table. After an hour of a match in which the correct goals expectation at kick-off was 2.8, the goals expectation for the remaining half-hour would be 1.1. If the game was still goalless, the appropriate price in the goals spread market would be 1.1. If one goal had been scored, it would be 2.1. And so on.

TRADING SYSTEMS Is there, some people wonder, a trading system you can follow during a game that will guarantee you a profit no matter what happens? Is it advisable, for example, to back the draw now on the fixed-odds betting exchanges and lay it later if the scores are still level?

I don't think so.

In essence, all trading systems are an attempt to back an event now and lay it later at a shorter price – or, alternatively, lay it now and back it later at a bigger price.

You will hear of trading systems that will give you a profit most times – but the other times a flaw in them will become apparent that is so big your losses will more than wipe out all of your earlier gains.

The obvious flaw in the draws idea is: what happens if someone scores after you have backed the draw but before you lay it?

In my opinion, all trading systems – no matter how ingenious they sound (and, believe me, some of them sound very ingenious indeed) – will fail ultimately unless one absolutely crucial condition is met. And that is that either the price at which you back or the price at which you lay – ideally, both – must be wrong and in your

WHAT IS THE CORRECT SUPREMACY EXPECTATION?

START OF MINUTE	PRE-MATCH SUPREMACY EXPECTATION:			
	0.50	1.00	1.50	2.00
1	0.50	1.00	1.50	2.00
6	0.48	0.96	1.44	1.92
11	0.46	0.92	1.38	1.84
16	0.44	0.87	1.31	1.74
21	0.41	0.83	1.24	1.65
26	0.39	0.78	1.16	1.55
31	0.36	0.73	1.09	1.45
36	0.34	0.68	1.01	1.35
41	0.31	0.62	0.93	1.25
46	0.28	0.56	0.84	1.12
51	0.26	0.51	0.76	1.02
56	0.23	0.45	0.68	0.90
61	0.20	0.39	0.59	0.79
66	0.17	0.34	0.50	0.67
71	0.14	0.27	0.41	0.55
76	0.11	0.21	0.32	0.43
81	0.08	0.15	0.23	0.30
86	0.04	0.09	0.13	0.18

favour – and, of course, by a sufficiently big margin to compensate for any commission you may have to pay.

In which case, why not simply attack the wrong price or prices?

If one of the two prices, either the opening one or the closing one, does not meet the condition all it does for you is reduce the profits you could eventually accumulate.

Let me give you an example of what I mean. It is a commonly-suggested trading system, though one that involves events that occur during the build-up to a match, before it goes in-play.

When England reach the finals of a major international tournament like the World Cup or European Championship, the odds on Three Lions victories usually – though not always – contract significantly in the hours before kick-off. The price gets squashed by a pile of patriotic pounds.

If you are sufficiently well-attuned to the public mood to be able to anticipate when these plunges will occur, you could probably make money, as many people have

WHAT IS THE CORRECT GOALS EXPECTATION?

START OF MINUTE	PRE-MATCH GOALS EXPECTATION:					
	2.20	2.40	2.60	2.80	3.0	3.20
1	2.20	2.40	2.60	2.80	3.00	3.20
6	2.12	2.31	2.50	2.69	2.89	3.08
11	2.02	2.20	2.39	2.57	2.76	2.94
16	1.92	2.09	2.27	2.44	2.62	2.79
21	1.82	1.98	2.15	2.31	2.48	2.64
26	1.71	1.86	2.02	2.17	2.33	2.48
31	1.60	1.74	1.89	2.03	2.18	2.32
36	1.49	1.62	1.76	1.89	2.03	2.16
41	1.37	1.50	1.62	1.74	1.87	1.99
46	1.23	1.34	1.46	1.57	1.68	1.79
51	1.12	1.22	1.32	1.42	1.52	1.63
56	1.00	1.09	1.18	1.27	1.36	1.45
61	0.87	0.95	1.03	1.10	1.18	1.26
66	0.74	0.80	0.87	0.94	1.01	1.07
71	0.60	0.66	0.71	0.77	0.82	0.88
76	0.47	0.51	0.55	0.60	0.64	0.68
81	0.33	0.36	0.39	0.42	0.45	0.48
86	0.20	0.21	0.23	0.25	0.27	0.28

suggested, by backing England when the market opens and laying them just before kick-off.

Because, by kick-off, the odds taken by England backers are usually badly wrong. The initial odds, most of the time, are also wrong, but not by as much.

So why not simply lay England at the most advantageous moment, which will normally be just before the referee whistles for play to commence? In the long run, I believe, you would be better off – though, admittedly, you could no longer hope to guarantee a profit on every single match.

It's a possibility that would have appealed to the proud Scotsman who at the start of this chapter exhorted us to examine all possibilities: Jock Stein. ▓

When watching TV can handicap golf profits

KEEPING UP WITH THE SCORE

MUCH DEPENDS ON HOW MUCH By PAUL KEALY
you enjoy watching so-called live sport
when it comes to exchange betting on golf.
For me, there is no better thrill than having
a few bets at long prices and then letting
the action unfold over four days on TV.

From the warm glow that you get from
seeing your man hit a four iron that rolls up
two feet from the pin for a gimme birdie to
the pulled drive out of bounds that sinks
your dreams of a big payday, you live every
shot. You urge your player towards great-
ness on each stroke while openly praying
for all manner of bad luck to strike anyone
who doesn't carry your dough. You can
leave the etiquette to the pros because
there is nothing quite like the joy of watching someone self-destruct in a moment of
high anxiety when you have laid them or
have backed the man most likely to benefit.

But if you want to make money out of in-
running golf betting on the American Tour
you have to forego all of that, stop watch-

ing TV and sit by your computer.

In short, you have to get Tourcast.

Tourcast is a quite extraordinary service offered by the PGA Tour and using their revolutionary ShotLink system. Here is part of the PGA Tour's description of what is in offer for the remarkably small fee of around $60 a year.

'Through lasers and wireless tracking devices, ShotLink tracks every shot in real-time to within inches. Tournament scoring is no longer limited to pars, birdies or bogeys. ShotLink provides the exact details for each and every shot: How far did he hit it? What is the distance to the pin? What is the player's lie or stance?'

Stats fans can also look up just about every tournament stat you can think of but the important phrase for in-running punters is 'real-time'. That's because we must get used to the fact that most of the sport we watch on TV is not as live as it is often claimed to be. And with American golf it is often not even close to being live.

Not only have you got the problem of relaying images from one part of the globe to the other, you also have to live with the fact the American sports coverage is two parts sport, one part ads. Roughly 20 minutes per hour is given over to advertisements and rarely a week goes by without Sky's excellent David Livingstone apologising for the constant interruptions.

Use of Tourcast gives you a chance to get ahead of your fellow punters.

And don't feel bad about it. This is not cheating. This information is available to anyone who cares to pay for it and you can bet your life that most bookmakers are using it when trading golf tournaments in-running.

Because you can only follow one group at a time on Tourcast (unless you have a bank of computers, which no doubt some big players do) you need to be in the right place at the right time, but here are a

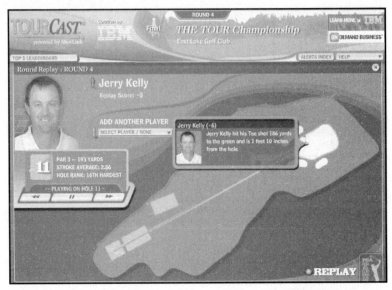

How Tourcast displayed news of Jerry Kelly's impending birdie

couple of examples of the sort of value bets you can expect to get.

The US Tour Championship in October 2004, featuring the top 30 players on the US Tour, looked highly likely to develop into a shootout between Tiger Woods and Retief Goosen. In the end it turned into a bit of a cakewalk for the Goose, but halfway through the final round things began to tighten up.

Jerry Kelly was one of the closers, so I started to monitor his progress more closely on Tourcast. And when he reached the par-three 11th hole, I was privileged to view, through some not very realistic graphics, his tee shot, after which followed a bubble saying: 'Jerry Kelly hit his tee shot 186 yards to the hole and is 1 feet [sic] 10 inches from the hole.'

He was six under at the time and the gimme birdie would take him to one stroke off leader Goosen. Clicking quickly over to Betfair's win market, I managed to place £20 at 24 and a further £50 at 18. Within seconds he had shortened to 14 and then 12.

a word of warning

 system overload

Having eulogised about the merits of Tourcast, if must be said that the service was less than perfect through much of 2005. This seems to be because the number of people using it has grown dramatically since they opened it up to customers from outside the USA.

There has been no end of problems with the service, but speed is easily the most annoying as if you are not getting the commentary in real time there is no point in using it. However, things were beginning to look up again in the summer and there is no doubt that Tourcast is massively important for betting in-running.

The basic Shotlink information is now also available on the pgatour.com main leaderboard, but while it could be considered a useful addition, the truth is it has made leaderboard updates even slower than before.

But this didn't just mean I had beaten the TV viewers because further shortening was to come. I had also been lucky enough to beat fellow Tourcast watchers, who were probably concentrating on the big two.

Unbelievably, it took Sky (no doubt via whichever US network was bombarding their viewers with ads) around five minutes to show Kelly's tee shot, at which point everyone wanted to get on. This meant I was able to lay back my stake at 8. In hindsight, of course, I should have laid back more than my stake because Kelly never looked likely to win thereafter, but the point is I put myself in with a chance of winning £800 for absolutely no risk at all.

As a golf nut I must confess that I rarely use Tourcast because I'd rather sit in front of my TV and watch the action unfold. I'm also privileged to work at the *Racing Post* in the presence of two people who in my view are among the finest golf betting judges in the country – Jeremy Chapman, whose verdicts you can read every Wednesday and Thursday, and Steve Palmer, who produces the excellent 19th Hole column every Tuesday. With those two on hand and my own more limited skills, I can enjoy all the action and still have a chance of backing some winners without spending hours in front of my PC and away from the action.

However, I began to realise how much my failure to use Tourcast was potentially costing me when punting on the Chrysler Classic of Tucson in February 2005.

This was the perfect Tourcast in-running punting medium because the TV cameras were instead focusing on the Accenture World Match Play final between David Toms and Chris DiMarco, and you could really narrow the field down to three or four possible winners with a few holes to play.

Eventual winner Geoff Ogilvy led for much of the final day, but a US Tour maiden never finds things easy and there was always likely to be a mishap on the way.

And so there was when, standing on the 15th tee with a one-stroke lead over Mark Calcavecchia, Ogilvy hooked his drive out of bounds. Quick as a flash, I managed to lay £500 of Ogilvy at 1.82 on Betfair. Unbelievably, he subsequently briefly traded at 1.66, but it was not long before I could get out of my position at the relatively juicy odds of 2.8 for a nice £200 profit whoever won. Ogilvy manfully made bogey at the 663-yard monster to retain a share of the lead but by then it didn't matter – or at least it shouldn't have.

It's one thing coming over all smug and telling you how easy it is to make money, but we all make mistakes and many punters have been known to hit the self destruct button through sheer greed. I am no different.

Instead of leaving it there, I suddenly decided that there were only two possible winners, Mark Calcavecchia and Ogilvy, who currently shared the lead. And so I chose to increase my win book for those two, not really caring how much the others cost as they had no chance anyway. The final hole was a 465-yard par-four averaging 4.3 and yielding only three birdies on the day so far, so there appeared little chance of the other so-called contender, Kevin Na, getting into a possible play-off.

That was mistake number one.

Mistake number two was leaving my PC to sort out a snack in the kitchen. Upon my return I was confronted by a Tourcast bubble saying: 'Kevin Na hit stroke 2 from the fairway and is 5 feet 2 inches from the hole.'

Suddenly I was confronted with a scenario in which I needed Ogilvy to sink a tricky little three-footer just to make a play-off with Calcavecchia and Na, who was costing me more than my potential winnings on the other two.

So what did I do? What a lot of people do when they lose the plot. Sweated profusely

Kevin Na sprang a surprise by making the Chrysler Classic play-off

and panicked. Several minutes of mis-trading ensued and the end result was a measly profit of £18.93.

It was a lesson learned – and hopefully not to be repeated even though I was never really in any danger of losing money – and one that all potential sports traders should take note of.

Being able to trade in and out of positions is something that is relatively new to fixed-odds punters. Spread bettors have been able to do it for years – albeit often at bad value prices given the spread firms' built-in profit margins – but it is something that most punters have very little experience of.

And if you decide you want to trade on an event it is imperative that you shed the punting mentality. First of all, if you are going to trade, you will soon find yourself doing it to stakes that are usually a good deal bigger than you are used to.

There is nothing wrong with starting small. It's easily the safest way of finding out whether you have the necessary skills to do it because it is not for everyone – never fall into the trap of thinking trading is a license to print money because, as always, there have to be losers to accommodate the winners.

But in the long run you will find that trading in fivers and tenners is going to result in a lot of button pressing for very little reward. The problems arise when the punting mentality takes over and you start making reckless calls you don't need to make. The result can often lead to you facing losses far greater than you would normally consider.

In the Tucson event you have just read about, Kevin Na was also a £200 winner for me at one stage, but so was every single player in the field, even those 15 strokes behind. I turned him into a hefty loser simply through greed and because the reckless punter in me took over.

There is nothing wrong with taking a view and simply having a bet, but you must beware of getting carried away when trading.

Now for a word of warning. As with any technology, hitches sometimes occur.

Sometimes Tourcast is slow, to the extent that it is actually behind the TV coverage. On other occasions it can crash, leaving everyone in the dark other than those listening to local radio coverage. And on others, the people transmitting the information can make mistakes. This can prove the most costly.

The classic Ford Championship final-round confrontation between Tiger Woods and Phil Mickelson in 2005 is a perfect example of how you can sometimes be put away.

Mickelson began the day two strokes clear of Woods and had maintained that advantage over the opening three holes, the pair sharing birdies at the first and then parring the next two.

Standing on the fourth tee, Mickelson

was trading at around 1.73 on Betfair. He soon got a lot shorter, though, as Woods missed the green on the long par three, only narrowly missing the water. Lefty hit his tee shot to around five feet according to Tourcast, who informed subscribers that Woods had barely moved his first chip from the rough, had made the green with his third shot and was facing an eight-footer just to drop one shot. The possibility of a three-shot swing loomed large and the only thing surprising about the betting moves was that Mickelson did not get any shorter than 1.3 on Betfair.

However, disaster was to strike for Mickelson backers, with Tourcast not only reporting that Woods had sunk the putt, but that it was for par and not bogey, while Lefty missed his for birdie so did not extend his lead even by a shot. The record books show that Tiger went on to beat his arch enemy in one of the most exhilarating final-round head-to-heads for years.

uncommon knowledge

 beware America's home-grown bias

Sometimes I wonder whether Tourcast is a good or a bad thing. I say this because the service crashed during the 2005 Players Championship at Sawgrass and it was plainly obvious that everyone was punting in the dark.

Some of the prices on offer to back or lay were scarcely believable. Take Steve Elkington, for instance. He was two shots off the lead with three holes to play, yet because so little was being shown by the US network of the two-time former champion, it seemed punters were prepared to believe he had blown his chance and he was trading at 160.

And when the cameras finally homed in on The Elk for his second at the par-five 16th, I was convinced that his approach was destined to find a watery grave. It didn't, though, as Elkington played a beauty to the edge of the green and got up and down for birdie.

Suddenly he was one off the pace and that 160 dropped to 14. Had Tourcast been running, you can bet that 160 would never have been available. It doesn't matter that Elkington did not win when you can trade with such big price discrepancies.

When a player is suddenly dropped from the TV coverage it is always easy to assume that he has also dropped out of contention. That is usually the case, but American TV producers tend to focus far more on home-grown players and they can often leave you in the dark about non-Americans even if they are right in the thick of battle. This is almost certainly what happened in the case of Elkington.

Tourcast used to be subscription-only via a credit card based in the USA, but it is open to all now and the more people who use it, the harder it will become to gain an edge. But Tourcast is not the be all and end all for golf punters and plenty of people are capable of making money out of in-running golf betting without using it.

For a start, Tourcast simply isn't available on the European Tour, whose website for so-called live scores is appalling by comparison with the US Tour. You are not going to get an edge in Europe via the internet, although you might with radio.

It's a recurring theme in this book, but it cannot be stated enough times that the big advantage of betting exchanges is that you get to take on players who have little idea of what they are doing.

Have a bet with a bookie, pre-event or in-running, and you can be sure that you are taking on an odds-compiler who has considered every possibility.

Betting in-running is not just about watching what is happening and then reacting. It's about being able to predict what is likely to happen next and arming yourself with as much information as possible to give you a chance of calling it correctly.

With golf, course knowledge is all-important, as those who waded into Paul Lawrie and Barry Lane for the Portuguese Open in 2005 were to learn. The pair were tied for the lead, two strokes clear of Paul Broadhurst with two holes to play at tricky Oitavos Golfe, and Broady was considered a no-hoper on Betfair, with the money centred on the leading pair.

That's fair enough you might think. But the final two holes at Oitavos Golfe promised to finish the season high on the list of hardest holes in Europe, if not ranked first and second. Both par fours were around 475 yards and after three rounds the 17th was averaging 4.48, with

uncommon knowledge

when layers fall behind

Having said that most major bookmakers are obviously using Tourcast, that doesn't mean you should swerve punting with them by using Betfair as your market guide, either for punting purposes or trading, especially for European Tour events.

Whether or not the local TV coverage is faster that the feed we receive from Sky, it appears pretty obvious from the market moves on Betfair that some punters, possibly even at the course, are getting the inside track before we do.

There is nothing more annoying than watching a price shorten and then seeing a putt holed a minute or so later. However, there are certain bookmakers who are slower than others in their reactions to the Betfair market, possibly because they are not following.

That means you can often get yourself into a trading position by punting with a bookmaker and laying at shorter odds on Betfair. There is little point in releasing the names of bookmakers who are slow to react as they will soon rectify the matter if they feel they are getting picked off. You will soon spot the ones.

the 18th a truly monstrous 4.71. You will see many par fives with a lower average.

Though it was hard to envisage Lawrie taking seven at 17 and Lane a nine at 18 (he also bogeyed 17), it was much easier to see the possibility of a play-off with Broadhurst being involved. Many punters got their fingers burned – Lane went as low as 1.13 – but those who did their homework made a killing.

But beware using the European Tour website for information. Rarely a tournament goes by without some players on the leaderboard being credited with birdies and eagles only for their scores to be corrected a few minutes later.

Many conspiracy theorists on the Betfair chatroom have questioned the integrity of the service, with some appearing adamant that some form of skulduggery is going on. Incompetence from youngsters being paid peanuts is the more logical answer, but whatever the case the European Tour website will cost you more money than you will make if you take everything as gospel.

Most of what you have read here concerns the as-it-happens action but there are obviously plenty of betting opportunities after every round and the Betfair market is normally at its strongest between rounds anyway.

I particularly like getting involved in the third and fourth rounds when the tournament has taken shape. Obviously you are unlikely to be getting on at massive prices unless you have an extreme view, but for trading purposes this is a good time to play – providing you call it right.

Depending on how you look at it, statistics can be extremely useful or thoroughly misleading. It is simply a case of interpreting them correctly.

Take putting stats for example. I find these are a particularly good guide to winner-finding on the final day of events, with most tournament winners finishing well inside the top ten for putts per green in regulation in the event.

The most basic information you can glean from this is that the player is putting well, but there is more to it than that.

A player with a terrific putts per GIR rank is either having a blinding day with the flat stick or his approach play is also excellent – and that is quite often the case.

And if a player has a bad rank for putts per GIR that can also tell you that his iron-play is not up to scratch. If a golfer is struggling with any particular part of his game, these problems normally unravel further during the high-pressure final rounds of tournaments.

On pgatour.com or europeantour.com you can get the basic statistical information but, not surprisingly, Tourcast does it better.

It can tell you not only how many putts he had during a round, but the total distance of all putts, the average distance the first putt missed by and the number of one putts and three-putts made.

The screen grab (above right) shows how 2005 Buick Open winner Vijay Singh fared on the greens through each round as he

Current Leader Vijay Singh (-24) Final STARTING HOLE: 1 TODAY: -2 AGE: 42 RESIDENCE: Fiji Islands, Unknown				SCORECARD	RESULTS	STATS
Player Statistics						
CATEGORIES	ROUND 1	ROUND 2	ROUND 3	ROUND 4	OVERALL
Around the Green					
Sand Saves	0.0%	100.0%	---	100.0%	83.3%
Scrambling	50.0%	75.0%	0.0%	100.0%	66.7%
Avg. Distance to Pin	9' 2"	5' 1"	5' 1"	10' 5"	7' 10"
On the Green					
Avg. Putts per GIR	1.357	1.643	1.471	1.933	1.600
One Putts	12	8	9	5	34
Three Putts	0	0	0	1	1
Lag Putts	1' 9"	2' 3"	1' 6"	2' 4"	2' 1"
Total Putting Distance	120' 1"	86' 9"	124' 2"	45' 11"	94' 3"
Distance Analysis					

How Tourcast broke down Vijay Singh's 2005 Buick Open putting stats

made his way to a comfortable four-stroke victory.

We can see from the first three rounds that he putted like a demon, but put in a much poorer effort on the final day. This was hardly surprising considering there was no need for him to attack.

Another useful stat is a player's final-round scoring average, although again you can't just take the numbers for granted.

There is no point smashing into a player based on a terrific final-round average of 68 if that figure has been gained by coming through the field from well off the pace in a pressure-free environment for a place just inside the top 20.

What is needed is a look at each individual player's record so you can see whether he was producing the goods when in contention.

A perfect example of this came in the 2005 US Bank Championship when Ben Crane led Scott Verplank by two strokes going into the final round, with a further three shots to the rest of the field.

Crane ranked seventh on final-round average for the year and had already posted some big finishes, while Verplank was 60th and had a long-established reputation for blowing winning chances.

Yet in what looked like being a two-horse race, Crane was available on Betfair at better than evens.

There are two reasons for this. First, Crane is extremely unpopular with golf viewers as he is one of the most painfully slow players on Tour and, from a punting perspective, you feel nervous for him every time he hovers over a shot. The truth is, though, that he is a highly competent finisher and proven winner.

The second, and more important, reason is that it can be argued that nearly all final-round leaders represent value on Betfair.

This is because there will be several punters who are on at big prices and are looking to hedge to guarantee a big profit. And the competition to hedge can be quite fierce, thus forcing the price out even further.

One thing is for certain, I have never seen one bookmaker come close to matching Betfair's price about the overnight final-round leader.

Even when VC went a standout 2-7 about Tiger Woods going into the third round of the 2005 Open at St Andrews (he was generally 1-6 elsewhere), the world No. 1 was freely available to several thousand pounds at 2-5 on Betfair. And he was 4-7 (1.57) on Betfair in the final round, when the best shop price was 2-5 (1.4).

Crane won without ever being challenged, but not all leaders do and the stats can guide you towards the right decisions.

Talking of best prices, it is probably fair to say that bookmakers rarely manage to beat the odds on offer on Betfair.

Take the 2005 Open at St Andrews and the price comparison published in the *Racing Post* on the eve of the tournament (see opposite). As you can see, Betfair was best about the vast majority of runners and

2005 OPEN CHAMPIONSHIP BACK & LAY PRICES

	Back		Lay		
	BFAIR	BDAQ	BFAIR	BDAQ	BEST BOOKIE
T Woods	4.2	4.2	4.3	4.3	4
E Els	12.5	12.5	13	13	11
V Singh	17	17	17.5	17.5	17
P Mickelson	21	21	22	22	19
S Garcia	23	23	24	24	23
R Goosen	25	25	26	26	23
L Donald	36	35	38	39	34
D Clarke	34	35	40	40	34
D Love	38	38	40	39	34
J Furyk	38	39	40	40	34
A Scott	40	40	42	41	34
L Westwood	55	50	60	60	46
D Toms	60	60	65	64	51
A Cabrera	60	64	65	72	51
M Campbell	70	70	75	78	67
T Clark	85	82	90	110	67
J Leonard	85	86	90	90	67
K Perry	85	90	90	100	81
C DiMarco	90	86	95	96	81
T Bjorn	100	102	110	120	67
M A Jimenez	110	110	120	130	101
S Appleby	100	120	110	130	101
N O'Hern	120	110	130	130	101
I Poulter	120	94	130	190	101
C Monty	130	104	140	130	101
J Daly	140	126	150	146	126
F Jacobson	140	140	150	150	126
S Cink	150	146	160	170	126
KJ Choi	170	150	180	170	101
J M Olazabal	160	144	170	180	126
G McDowell	170	160	180	200	126
T Immelman	180	166	190	200	126
R Allenby	230	180	240	250	151
F Couples	230	230	250	350	151
T Hamilton	270	270	280	385	201
S Ames	290	300	310	350	151

markedly so, even taking into account the effect of commission.

Of course, Betfair's outright market is winner only, but Betdaq offer each-way betting (albeit to lower odds than you can get on Betfair), while you can bet place only as well, although liquidity is sometimes threadbare.

Finally, there can be great value at the death of a tournament if you can keep in your head a mental picture of what has happened before. If a player is standing over a putt to win, what are the chances of him making it? If you have been watching all day, the chances are you will have seen the same putt several times.

Indeed, the commentators quite often do the job for you, and you will regularly hear things like: "This breaks more than you think. Virtually every putt from here today has missed right/left, come up short," etc.

But if a player is facing a tricky eight-footer he is normally trading at long odds-on, say around 1.3. If you lay it and he misses, you are in trading heaven with a play-off to come.

You can even put up even shorter prices in-running while hovering over the cancel button as you will be amazed at how many people will go low in anticipation of the putt dropping only to see it miss.

It most famously happened in 2004 when Justin Leonard was backed at 1.01 as his putt to win was on the way to the hole.

It missed, Singh went on to win the play-off, and the punter responsible later went on to the Betfair chatroom to own up, blaming it on his cat for jumping on to his keyboard. ■

how to snooker fellow punters

ON CUE TO TRAP MUGS

ONE OF THE RECURRENT THEMES   By PAUL KEALY
of this book is that betting on exchanges
allows you to take on other punters rather
than professional odds-makers.

Whether you agree or not, the vast
majority of punters are mugs. It's why
bookmakers have had it so good so for so
long and why shrewder players have made
profits beyond their wildest dreams
through exchange betting.

Having watched most of the action at the
2005 World Championships it has to be
said that snooker has its fair share of
punting clowns.

Indeed, if you want to trade any sport in-
running, I defy you to lose money on
snooker. In many cases you really need
know little about the sport.

Let's take, for instance, the quarter-final
between Shaun Murphy and Steve Davis.
Murphy had been all the rage the night
before the match, having seen off John
Higgins in some style. By morning he was
trading at around 1.3 to back on Betfair,
with Davis 3.9.

Once the contest got under way, all
unmatched bets were cancelled as usual
and the market turned in-play. That's when
things got interesting.

Steve Davis shortened despite looking like falling behind

Murphy, on a break of around 30, had shortened slightly (1.27 to back) but there wasn't much in it. However, there was not much money on either the back or lay side for Davis – the shorter-priced runner is usually the focus of in-running attention, which is why sometimes you can see chunks of money traded at 1.01 on the favourite, but not see anyone taking bigger than that 33-1 on the outsider – leaving the opportunity for someone to put up a ludicrously short price in the hope of getting matched.

And that's what happened. Someone was lured into backing Davis, who at this time was odds-on to go 1-0 down, at 3.3. We should not be too disparaging about casual punters who log on for an interest and a small bet, but the truth is they are rarely price sensitive and struggle to understand the mechanics of backing and laying.

In a two-runner race like snooker, a back of one player is the same as a lay of the other, yet someone took 3.3 Davis – shorter than was available at the start despite the

Nugget looking certain to fall behind – when 1.28 Murphy was on offer to lay. In other words 2.3-1 was taken about someone freely available on the same screen at around 3.5-1.

That's one example of what can happen in snooker match betting, but the really easy money is to be made on Betfair's in-running frame-by-frame markets.

These are markets that don't carry much liquidity as not many people play in them. However, they do seem to attract enough punters prepared to throw good money after bad and, of course, enough traders to accommodate them.

Because many punters are not price sensitive, they have little concept of value. And that in turn means layers can offer prices that would make your average tight-fisted bookmaker squirm with embarrassment. In a two-runner race in which each has an equal chance you can expect bookmakers to offer something like 5-6 the pair. Yet in markets with little liquidity you can often get away with offering far worse percentages, although probably not before the action begins. And that's when the real fun starts anyway.

There is a popular misconception in snooker that most frames are won with a single contribution from the first player to get a chance, and this manifests itself in some astonishing frame betting market moves.

I'll give you just one example of the sort of fluctuations that are typical in these markets. The quarter-final between Matthew Stevens and Stephen Hendry could not have been tighter. It was 10-9 to Hendry and both players had been backed at evens to win frame 20 before the break-off.

Yet within seconds of potting the opening red, Hendry was on offer at just 1.68. After moving to a total of five the Scot was down to 1.56, at 18 he was 1.3 and when hit 40 he was matched at 1.25 before missing a black.

But this was only a cue for punters to go

uncommon knowledge

 spotting an overreaction

Taking advantage of other peoples' over-reactions is one of the easiest ways to make money out of any sport and a fine example of this can be taken from a 2005 Premier League snooker match between Paul Hunter and Steve Davis.

Hunter was a long odds-on favourite for the match, with Davis trading at the off at 4.4 – just under 7-2. Yet during a break of 36 in the opening frame Davis was backed at all rates down to evens. That he went on to win the frame – and the match 4-2 – is totally irrelevant. Whoever took the evens and prices similar had over-reacted to the nth degree and snapped up some serious bad value.

For the record, Davis broke down on 36 and had drifted back out to 4.2 before a Hunter mistake let the Nugget back in to take a 1-0 lead. However, even at 1-0, Davis was on offer at 2.75. Those who laid the evens were in position to make free money by backing him back.

Stevens mad. Having made the most of an easy opening, the Welshman was already backed at evens despite trailing by 39 points. With a cluster of red balls tight on the pink, and one sitting next to the yellow, this was hardly a gilt-edged opportunity, yet by the time Stevens had reached 20, he was being backed at 1.49.

In the very next frame, a typically nervy Crucible encounter, Stevens was traded at 1.1 and Hendry at 1.41 before the colours, by which time both were hovering around the evens mark.

Yes, Stevens did miss an unusually easy black to hand the initiative back to Hendry, but simple pots being missed are far more commonplace than people imagine. The fact is that you have to play ridiculously well and have a degree of luck with the splitting of the reds to sew up a frame with one visit.

Hendry is the most prolific century break-maker in the game with approaching 700 career tons by the end of 2005. Yet he is miles clear of everyone else in the lists and few current players have recorded more than 150 centuries in their careers.

In most frames both players will get a chance, and when that happens they tend to trade at odds that are far shorter than they realistically should be. Yet because punters continually over-react, both players in a snooker match are likely to trade at significant odds-on in two frames out of three and the trading possibilities are endless.

On semi-finals day in the World Championship I spent a marathon day trading frame-by-frame markets. In all, I sat through 16 frames and made a profit on 14 of them. And the beauty of it was that I wasn't doing anything that could be remotely described as shrewd. All I was doing was taking the contrary view – that the person in the balls should be laid rather than backed.

It may well be that I hit a certain stage of the tournament in which pressure was

Matthew Stevens on his way to beating Jimmy White at Sheffield

more in evidence, but I am totally convinced that you will make decent money simply by fielding against punters who over-react to a frame-winning chance. Without doubt my favourite frame in the tournament was one in which Stevens was traded at 1.25 after potting the opening red. A subsequent missed blue saw him back out to 2.5.

During the World Championships Betfair treated all frame-by-frame markets as 'in-play' even though they hadn't started. This means that no unmatched bets were cancelled at the break-off. This is unusual because it puts even more onus on punters to monitor their positions, but it does allow you to put loads of orders up and then sit back and let the action unfold.

I am 99.9 per cent certain that if you put up 1.5 for either player in every frame you will find yourself matched on both sides more than enough times to cover for the times that you are not. By putting up 1.5 you only need to see 50 per cent of bets matched on both sides to draw even, while the shorter the price you offer initially, the less successful you need to be. By offering 1.25 you only need a 25 per cent success rate.

Beware, though, you have to be careful how much money you put up. At the time of writing, these markets were not the most popular around. Stick up too much and you will only get fully matched on the player who wins. These are markets in which you can make a small amount of money with some basic trading.

ANTE-POST MARKETS Betting on the outright winner of the snooker tournament is not something I have been a fan of, largely because all the usual suspects are priced very defensively by the layers.

However, things are changing. Whether the standard is falling at the top end or improving at the bottom – probably the latter – there is now more competition than ever before and outsiders have a genuine chance of making an impact.

Sussing out which ones to back takes some homework, but studying the draw and spotting potentially vulnerable big guns – those who might be under pressure for rankings points or who have had a poor season – can lead to you uncovering some nuggets among the rags.

And remember, when backing underdogs on Betfair you will usually be getting far greater value than with the bookmakers – and if they do progress and more top players fall by the wayside you can lock yourself in a tidy profit. ▪

how to exploit illiquid markets

RUGBY UNION AND LEAGUE

THERE IS ONE BIG PERCEIVED negative about betting on rugby league and union on the exchanges, and although there is a simple way to eradicate it the current situation also opens up new avenues for potential traders.

By DAVID BARKER

One of the most oft-levelled criticisms of exchange betting is poor liquidity. Some would argue that it's all right an exchange boasting about welcoming winners and not limiting bet sizes, but what are the attractions if you can't find someone else willing to lay you a decent bet at a fair price, let alone at the much-trumpeted 20 per cent over the odds?

Ignoring for a moment the fact that some bookmakers (for they are often the critics) have a less than impeccable reputation when it comes to laying their advertised prices, it is a fair point. There is certainly a lack of market depth in some of the lesser-traded sports and among those are rugby union and league.

The various rugby match odds markets are listed on Betfair five days in advance and the weekend handicap lines normally on a Thursday, but outside of high-profile games there is precious little money available in them until near kick-off time. And for non-live matches the cash and bet requests sometime don't arrive at all.

But surely the punters that complain are in a position to do something about these illiquid markets? If no prices are available on a market, then request some – after all, that is the beauty of betting exchanges.

If you are not happy with what you are being offered, then request your own prices, however defensive or fanciful you may think they are. If you don't ask, then you certainly won't get, and the five-year history of Betfair is littered with proof that occasionally you will get filled at some extraordinary and unexpected prices.

If only a handful of Betfair's rugby punters did this, the markets would take off sooner rather than later. Liquidity breeds liquidity. However, if they do you could be missing an ideal opportunity to secure a brilliant "green" before the match kicks off.

It may simply be the case that the demand for rugby is not particularly high, but only the narrow-minded will see that as a disadvantage.

HOW TO MAKE ILLIQUID/EMPTY MARKETS WORK FOR YOU

Most people think there is nothing more off-putting than clicking into a market and seeing it empty, but that is actually when others start to lick their lips.

After all, it is not often a punter gets the chance to be first to price up an event. And for those venturing into it on Betfair knowing a fair bit about the sport and punting, there is money to be made.

The beauty of an empty market on an exchange is that you are not limited as to what prices you can offer. There will be no-one tapping you on the shoulder and saying you should be ashamed of yourself by pricing it up to 150-plus per cent.

You put up what prices you will be happy to lay come what may, safe in the knowl-

Bourgoin fielded a weakened team when losing to Leinster

edge that the other punters don't know who the would-be shark is.

And, remember, there is also probably another good reason why the market is empty – most other punters don't know what the odds should be. And this is where you have a potential goldmine.

You have only to click in any Betfair market and look up price histories of the runners to see that fortune often favours the punters who are first to offer or request odds – some of the outlandish prices matched at the start of the graph often make pretty grim reading for layers.

There is one particular rugby union match that sticks in my mind and highlights the value to be had of going in first.

Bourgoin fielded a virtual reserve side (they rested 12 regulars) for their visit to Lansdowne Road in the European Cup group stages in December 2004, and were promptly humiliated by a Leinster side running in 13 tries and racing to a 92-17 victory.

There was widespread condemnation of

the French outfit in the aftermath of that victory – it wasn't the first time in the competition that they had put out such an under-strength side – and there were immediate rumours that the competition's organisers were going to meet to discuss Bourgoin's tactics.

That had all bookmakers fighting shy of pricing up Bourgoin's fixture the following week – at home to the same Leinster side – but one punter I know could not wait for Betfair to get the market up. He sensed easy money.

The reason? First, he knew the market would be a blank canvas for him to work on and it was obvious that most punters were going to over-react to the result and want to get with Leinster in the pre-match markets.

And, more importantly, Bourgoin were lying second in the highly-competitive French First Division – a league that also featured the might of Toulouse, Biarritz, Perpignan and Stade Francais – and boasted a proud and formidable domestic home record over the years.

If they had been given a stern warning by the European Cup organisers and told to field their strongest XV, they should have been no bigger than 2.5 to win the reverse fixture – and possibly even favourites.

But this punter was sure he could lay Leinster at a lot shorter than 1.66 in the match, and he couldn't wait for Betfair to get their market up. Once they had obliged, in he stepped, chancing his arm with an offer to lay £1,000 of Leinster at 1.14 – if you don't ask, you don't get.

Imagine his complete disbelief when he logged in the next morning to find that someone had bitten and backed Leinster with him at 1.14 – not just a tenner but the entire £1,000 had gone. In fact, although the punter was full of glee, he was also slightly gutted that he hadn't put up more.

In the match itself, Bourgoin went off at

about 3.6 to win – and Leinster at 1.41 – after recalling many of their first team and were highly unfortunate not to win the game. Bourgoin traded at 1.3 in running before a late Brian O'Driscoll try saw the Irish side edge a 26-23 victory.

But even before the opening whistle, the punter could clearly have guaranteed himself a three-figure "all green" book.

There is one other market that punters should focus on pre-match as well. We will look at that next before turning our attention to in-running strategies.

It is clearly impossible to provide any firm strategies about match odds and handicap betting in a book of this nature, as team news is all important in any such punts.

As we have seen in recent seasons with St Helens (players rested) and Wigan (squad decimated by injuries), punters should clearly hold fire if there is any suggestion that a team is going to put out a massively under-strength side – unless, of course, you get reliable information first and can snaffle up some fancy odds and lenient handicaps about their opponents.

But there is an avenue in which some punters have consistently made big profits recently – by laying the prohibitive odds-on match favourites to be leading at half-time and full-time.

The logic that underpins this lay is simple, but it is unbelievable what prices backers are willing to take on this market.

Rugby union and league are intensely physical and attritional sports and the class chasm that separates some sides tends to become apparent only after the lesser teams have been softened up in the opening exchanges.

This may take 40 minutes or possibly even 60, because allied to the class advantage there is very often an eventual physical superiority, too.

Basically, lesser sides can excel and live

uncommon knowledge

'all green' is perfect book

Contrary to what some punters might tell you, 'all green' is not a dog track in Birmingham. It is the term used by punters who have traded their way into a position that guarantees them a profit whatever the result of the market they are betting in.

It is called 'all green' because the market you have traded will show a profit figure under every selection and this will appear in green type.

Potential losses are shown in red, so being 'all red' means that you have got into such a mess that you can only lose.

with their opponents until they run out of gas – but this does not seem to be reflected in the Betfair half-time/full-time markets.

Let's take Super League, for instance. The 2005 season is littered with examples where 1.12 or shorter match odds favourites have failed to be leading at half-time and full-time.

Let's start with Leeds, the domestic dominant force. They tend to pour it on late and by the end of June 2005 had failed to be in front at the interval in four games; two matches against St Helens (drawing 18-18 before winning 30-18; and losing the other game 38-24), Wakefield (losing 22-6 before going down 44-28 – the shock of the season), and Hull (drawing 12-12 before winning 34-14).

And, in another five games, they were only in front at the interval by six points or less, pretty uncomfortable stuff for their ht-ft (half time-full time) backers, at odds regularly in the 1.15 territory against the poorer sides and at the 1.35 mark when at home to higher-quality teams such as Hull.

These may not be eye-popping stats, but we need to remember that in 2005 Leeds were the best and physically strongest team in Super League.

St Helens, the second best team in the League, were down or level against the following teams at half-time before avoiding defeat on the full-time whistle: Warrington, Huddersfield (twice), Widnes, Salford and London – hardly a roll call of the best sides in the top flight and there were some expensive failures there for the ht-ft money buyers.

And even whipping boys Leigh had been be in front at half-time twice against Warrington in the 2005 season – once they were 7-4 up before losing 42-7. They also provide one of the best examples themselves too, as they were 8-6 down at the turnaround against First Division Halifax in the Challenge Cup before winning 40-20.

Jonny Wilkinson is tackled in the 25-25 draw with Argentina in 2005

Throw in the likes of Toulouse blitzing 1.16 favourites Widnes in the Challenge Cup quarter-final, and you can clearly see this is an avenue to be explored.

You may have to endure the odd five-match losing spell but, at the prices involved, you can tolerate that.

Sooner rather than later you will hit a jackpot such as the Leeds-Wakefield match, where Leeds were matched at 1.04 to be leading at half-time and full-time. And I'd be inclined to narrow it down further by taking on the big teams when they are a short price on the road.

You don't have to tell rugby union punters on Betfair of the attractions of laying their sides to be leading at half-time and full-time.

The 2005 British and Irish Lions are a classic example. They were backed at 1.04 in that market when 40-plus point favourites against a second-string Argentina at Twickenham pre-tour, only to be behind at the interval and struggling to salvage a 25-25 draw.

And that theme continued in New Zealand, with the Lions going in at the break drawing 17-17 with Bay of Plenty, losing 7-6 to Taranaki – matches they eventually won well but for which they were massive odds-on favourites – and then level with Otago 13-13 in a later match.

Of course, once you highlight the value in a market that value tends to disappear. But check it out. There is an associated in-running hedge to be gleaned from playing this market as well, what I could call potential "double cop" scenario if the market goes in your favour early in the match.

IN-RUNNING BETTING Rather like match odds and handicap recommendations, it is pretty much impossible to give in-running advice in a book of nature; what works for some clearly will not for others and you have to react to the game unfolding in front of you, as you see it. It's your money, after all.

But for what it is worth I will outline the in-running strategy that works for me, starting off, as promised, with the in-running hedging trade linked to the half-time full-time market lay.

For those who do lay the favourite in that market, there is an ideal scenario – the outsider taking a big early lead. Let's take possibly the most extreme rugby example in Betfair's history – the Lions v Argentina match in Cardiff in May 2005.

In that match it was easy to lay the Lions-Lions double result pre-match at 1.05 and 1.06, and plenty got filled at 1.04.

The Argentinians were without virtually all their star players but they really took it to a disjointed Lions side and opened up an early 13-0 lead in the opening quarter, at which point the pre-match ht-ft layers had a decision to make.

Did they sit with their (now very attractive) bet, or did they close out that position at the revised odds of 1.1 Lions in the match odds line – locking in a very handsome no-lose profit by backing the home side in that 80-minute market – and hope for a "double cop"?

The decision of if/when to act, or hedge, is entirely dependent on your own view about how the match is going. But I would always be inclined to at least minimise any loss in the ht-ft market by backing that liability back in the match odds market at the available bigger odds.

I say "double cop" because anybody closing out at this stage could still clearly win on both bets. The Lions could fight back to be only losing 13-12 at the break, at which point the half-time full-time lay would be a winner, but the hedging back bet of the Lions at 1.1 would probably now be a 1.03 chance – as the Lions were 40-point handicap favourites and would be expected to cut loose, make their class tell and comfortably win the match.

Punters who hedged would now be in a superb position to further trade into an even better green book, or simply sit tight and hope for a Lions win and that double cop.

As it happens, backers of the Lions in the match odds market would have lost out on that side of the bet – though that loss would have been more than covered by the successful ht-ft lay – as they only drew 25-25.

But this admittedly extreme example clearly illustrates the trading potential of taking such a low-risk, pre-match position. If you had done this in St Helens' Super League matches (see previous statistics) you would have double copped rather handsomely as they staged their winning comebacks in several games after going in down at half-time.

And it is arguably more relevant in rugby league matches, in which teams can put three tries on the opposition in quick succession.

In the aforementioned Toulouse-Widnes match it was possible to lay the Widnes-Widnes double result at 1.36. But in the match odds market just 20 minutes into the game, with the French side 20-0 up, it was possible to lay Toulouse in the win market at 1.61.

All punters have what I class a Plan A, i.e. they know who they think will win and bet accordingly. I would strongly suggest that punters think about what their Plan B is if the match doesn't go as they foresee.

It's okay backing Leeds at 1.02 to beat Wakefield, and at 1.04 in the ht-ft market, but where do you go trading-wise if things go badly wrong?

I'll tell you where – deep into trouble, then further down.

Sometimes, you have to consider the trading aspect of a bet before you consider who will win. Back or lay what you think will leave you in the best possible trading position for the least risk. It sounds illogical, but in my experience it will steer you away from some horrendous short-priced failures.

As I said earlier, actual in-running strategies are impossible to generalise upon but here are two last tips that work for me.

If you are betting in running, always look to consistently lay both teams in a 100 per cent or higher book; do not back unless the price is so attractive that you can't let it pass.

Remember, most exchange punters are still backers-only and they'll more often than not take a bad back price that is readily available.

That may sound like a fanciful notion but in relatively illiquid, fast-moving markets you will find you can lay both teams to the tune of 110 per cent-plus on occasions quite easily.

The upshot of this is that you will have a massive green on the draw towards the end of the match and, if the game is tight, the potential of laying off some of this profit at short odds to ensure a handsome all-win book.

You may have to pay over-the-odds to get the lay done late on – as those who laid the draw at 2.5 before Jonny Wilkinson took that game-equalling kick in the Argentina-Lions match found out (it should have been about 1.15 given his kicking record), but if you sit tight and the draw comes in, it is big money for no risk.

And if you are laying in-running, this is another favourite ploy of mine: if a team is on the opposition line, everyone wants to back them. So put up a price you would be willing to lay even if the attacking team scores. You will be amazed how many times you get filled without the team actually scoring. ■

How to be ace
at tennis trading

ON GUARD
FOR NET
PROFITS

By JAMES
PYMAN

TENNIS MATCHES ARE IDEAL FOR in-running trading and it is no surprise that Betfair reported a 100 per cent increase in turnover from Wimbledon between 2004 and 2005.

In contrast to sports such as football and rugby, in which contests are played out over a designated period, tennis matches have no fixed time limit with the victor being the first player to win a certain number of points – in theory the minimum number in a best-of-three-sets contest that doesn't involve any deuces would be 48.

But crossing the winning line is never easy and the tennis scoring system opens up the possibility for players to stage comebacks from the most unlikely positions.

It's also common for there to be wild swings in momentum during matches, particularly in women's singles contests where breaks of serve are more frequent – and that means massive fluctuations in the odds of the players, which is the dream scenario for exchange traders.

MATCH TRADING STRATEGIES

Price fluctuations during matches are driven by the outcome of individual or series of points and the degree to which the market swings in response to these passages of play is controlled by their potential to influence the fate of games, sets and the match.

The outcome of the first point of a match is unlikely to alter the odds by a single hundredth but the result of a set point could dramatically change the complexion of the market.

Each individual point provides only a brief snapshot of the contest and therefore it's usually hard to formulate any concrete ideas on how a match is likely to unfold from analysing a single point.

Another potential problem with point-by-point trading is that it's easy to get engrossed in the action unfolding in front of you, which can result in you subconsciously developing a bias to either of the players that will influence your decision-making processes.

Watch the market during a fiercely-contested Grand Slam match. One brilliant shot can shave a few hundredths off the price even if it does not lead to a game-winning chance.

A broader image of how a match is developing can be gleaned from scrutinising the way games unravel. For example, the first few games often provide an insight into how players are coping with each other's styles – which can be a major factor in determining who emerges victorious.

The way sets evolve provide a more vivid insight into the destiny of the match (see player profile section on page 151), but whether you want to trade after each point, game or set it is paramount that you develop a clear strategy before the match starts and it can be a big advantage to arm yourself with statistics relevant to in-running such as players' records in

GENERAL IN-RUNNING PATTERNS AT THE US OPEN (2000-04)

	A	B	A %	B%	A Odds	B Odds
A	392	112	77.8	22.2	(2-7)	(7-2)
AA	320	16	95.2	4.8	(1-20)	(20-1)
AAB	64	16	80.0	20.0	(1-4)	(4-1)
AABB	10	16	38.5	61.5	(13-8)	(8-13)
AB	72	99	42.1	57.9	(11-8)	(8-11)
ABA	58	12	82.9	17.1	(1-5)	(5-1)
ABAB	14	12	53.8	46.2	(5-6)	(6-5)
ABB	13	87	13.0	87.0	(7-1)	(1-7)
ABBA	13	16	44.8	55.2	(6-5)	(5-6)

GENERAL IN-RUNNING PATTERNS AT WIMBLEDON (2000-04)

	A	B	A %	B %	A Odds	B Odds
A	401	97	80.5	19.5	(1-4)	(4-1)
AA	313	10	96.9	3.1	(1-30)	(30-1)
AAB	70	10	87.5	12.5	(1-7)	(7-1)
AABB	18	10	64.3	35.7	(4-7)	(7-4)
AB	88	87	50.2	49.8	(Evs)	(Evs)
ABA	65	18	78.3	21.7	(2-7)	(7-2)
ABAB	21	18	53.8	46.2	(5-6)	(6-5)
ABB	23	69	25.0	75.0	(3-1)	(1-3)
ABBA	23	10	69.7	30.3	(2-5)	(5-2)

GENERAL IN-RUNNING PATTERNS AT AUSTRALIAN OPEN (2000-04)

	A	B	A %	B %	A Odds	B Odds
A	375	132	74.0	26.0	(1-3)	(3-1)
AA	307	29	91.4	8.6	(1-10)	(10-1)
AAB	62	29	68.1	31.9	(1-2)	(2-1)
AABB	14	29	32.6	67.4	(2-1)	(1-2)
AB	84	99	45.9	54.1	(6-5)	(5-6)
ABA	66	15	81.5	18.5	(1-5)	(5-1)
ABAB	12	15	44.4	55.6	(6-5)	(5-6)
ABB	18	84	17.6	82.4	(9-2)	(2-9)
ABBA	18	15	54.5	45.5	(5-6)	(6-5)

KEY (for all): A=player who won first, B=player who lost first set, e.g ABB=player A won first set but and B won the next two, A%=percentage of matches won by player who won first set, B%=percentage of matches won by player who lost first set.

GENERAL IN-RUNNING PATTERNS AT FRENCH OPEN (2000-04)						
	A	B	A %	B%	A Odds	B Odds
A	385	123	75.8	24.2	(1-3)	(3-1)
AA	282	28	91.0	9.0	(1-10)	(10-1)
AAB	72	28	72.0	28.0	(2-5)	(5-2)
AABB	16	28	36.4	63.6	(7-4)	(4-7)
AB	90	92	49.5	50.5	(Evs)	(Evs)
ABA	72	19	79.1	20.9	(1-4)	(4-1)
ABAB	11	19	36.7	63.3	(7-4)	(4-7)
ABB	18	73	19.8	80.2	(4-1)	(1-4)
ABBA	18	18	50.0	50.0	(Evs)	(Evs)

KEY (for all): A=player who won first, B=player who lost first set, e.g ABB=player A won first set but and B won the next two, A%=percentage of matches won by player who won first set, B%=percentage of matches won by player who lost first set.

deciding sets and tie-breaks which can provide vital clues as to how matches will unfold.

SURFACE The surface a match is being contested on can influence the general way in which matches unfold, but this only seems to be significant in lengthier best-of-five-sets contests.

Consequently it's essential that you tailor your in-running betting to the terrain type in Grand Slam and Davis Cup matches.

The tables show the way matches progressed on clay, grass and hard courts for all main-tour best-of-three-sets matches between 2000 and 2004 and the patterns in the three tables are strikingly similar.

As you would expect, winning the first set is a big advantage and across all three surfaces just over 80 per cent of players went on to win after pocketing the opening set.

The momentum a player gains from recovering from a set down to level proceedings appears to be worth around two per cent as on each terrain around 52 per cent of those who recovered from losing the first set by squaring the match at 1-1 then took the decider.

But matches have tended to evolve differently at the four Grand Slams in the period 2000-2005.

Front runners have been tougher to stop in their tracks at Wimbledon compared with the three other majors as it appears to be much more difficult to change the dynamics of the match on grass, where the points are short and deny the player who is behind the chance to find his rhythm.

At the All England Club 80.5 per cent of those who won the first set won their matches but this figure drops to 77.8 at the US Open, 75.8 a the French Open and 74 at the Australian Open. This trend is also apparent when you examine the conversion rates of players from 2-0 up – Wimbledon 96.9 per cent success from this position, US Open 95.2, Australian Open 91.4 and French Open 91.

Comebacks from precarious positions are more likely to occur on the slow clay at Roland Garros or the medium-paced Rebound Ace courts in Melbourne than the pace-laden grass at the All England Club or the lively Decoturf at Flushing Meadow. This strongly suggests that more dramatic shifts in momentum occur on slow surfaces and is something in-running punters should monitor closely.

PLAYER PROFILING It's important to have a good understanding of the general way matches develop, but it must be remembered that players possess unique physical and mental characteristics so each match must be approached differently.

Therefore, it is useful to get inside players' minds. We can do this by monitoring and recording how they respond to different situations. Certain players are almost impossible to peg back after winning the first set, but others struggle to race away with matches once in front and are more likely to be reeled in.

Some respond positively to being a set down, while others drop their heads and are easily rolled over.

A prime example is Lleyton Hewitt, who has a reputation of being a fierce fighter who is not one to shirk a battle and his record from 1-0 down reinforces this status.

Between 2000 and June 2005 the Australian won 48.8 per cent of his matches after losing the opening set – and that is a phenomenal record when you consider the average win rate from 1-0 down for players ranked inside the top 100 during that period is 22 per cent.

Building up a database of how players have fared when winning or losing sets at various stages of matches is an invaluable in-running tool, providing an insight into their personality and mental toughness and it allows you to formulate a clear game plan before the match starts.

For example there could be a match involving Player A who has a relatively poor record from 1-0 up against Player B, who has proved he is better than most at coming back from a set down.

If Player A wins the first set it could be worth backing Player B, who will have drifted considerably from his starting price, but has in the past shown what it takes to recover from an early setback and is facing a player who has shown in the past that he struggles to win matches when in an advantageous position.

PRESSURE SITUATIONS Particularly when two evenly-matched players go head-to-head, the fate of matches is often determined by the outcome of pressure situations such as break-points, tie-breaks and final sets.

It's therefore important to know how different players usually deal with these tense episodes of play. Here we look at some of these situations.

GENERAL IN-RUNNING PATTERNS IN BEST-OF-THREE-SETS HARD-COURT MATCHES (2000-04)

	A	B	A %	B%	A Odds	B Odds
A	4666	1092	81.0	19.0	(1-4)	(4-1)
B	1092	4666	19.0	81.0	(4-1)	(1-4)
AB	941	1086	46.4	53.6	(6-5)	(5-6)
BA	1086	941	53.4	46.4	(5-6)	(6-5)

GENERAL IN-RUNNING PATTERNS IN BEST-OF-THREE-SETS CLAY-COURT MATCHES (2000-04)

	A	B	A %	B%	A Odds	B Odds
A	3452	743	82.3	17.7	(2-9)	(9-2)
B	743	3452	17.7	82.3	(9-2)	(2-9)
AB	1887	2187	46.3	53.7	(6-5)	(5-6)
BA	2187	1887	53.7	46.3	(5-6)	(6-5)

GENERAL IN-RUNNING PATTERNS IN BEST-OF-THREE-SETS GRASS-COURT MATCHES (2000-04)

	A	B	A %	B%	A Odds	B Odds
A	716	156	82.1	17.9	(2-9)	(9-2)
B	156	716	17.9	82.1	(9-2)	(2-9)
AB	143	155	48.0	52.0	(11-10)	(10-11)
BA	155	143	52.0	48.0	(10-11)	(11-10)

KEY (for all): A=player who won first, B=player who lost first set, e.g AB=player A won first set but B won second set, A%=percentage of matches won by player who won first set, B%=percentage of matches won by player who lost first set.

THE FIFTH SET What is interesting about the final set of a best-of-five-sets match is that unless a player has battled back from two sets down – in which case he has on average gone on to win around 66 per cent of final sets (except at Wimbledon where sample size in the table is small) – the outcome of the decider doesn't appear to be dramatically influenced by the events of the four previous sets.

But commonly the player who was

favourite at the start of the contest, especially if they were long odds-on at the outset, is seen by the layers and on the exchanges as the most likely winner of the fifth set.

However, there is no relationship between ability and success in the fifth set of a marathon. Some players thrive in these situations, while others invariably come up short. For example three-time Wimbledon champion Roger Federer's career five-set record up to the end of June 2005 was just a modest eight wins from 16 matches.

It therefore makes sense when matches spill over into a fifth set to side with players with strong final-set records who have proved they have the requisite stamina, strength and mental toughness to emerge triumphant from a marathon.

TIE-BREAKS These occur with greater frequency on speedier surfaces such as grass, on which service breaks are harder to achieve with approximately one in every four ATP tour grass-court matches since 2001 featuring a tie-break.

Most players' success rates in tie-breaks throughout their careers are between 45 and 55 per cent.

However, some possess records that fall outside this band and they seem to thrive or crumble in these nerve-jangling situations, so knowing the respective tie-break records of two players can assist in-running bettors.

BREAK-POINTS These are more common on clay than faster surfaces as the serve is less of a weapon on sluggish red dirt. Nevertheless, even on clay players with big serves tend to stave off a higher percentage of break-points as if they conjure up a heavy first delivery they will invariably win the point.

The best returners convert more of their break-point opportunities.

OUTRIGHT BETTING Providing your outright selection negotiates the early stages you will invariably have the option to guarantee a profit by laying them back at shorter prices.

It's common for tournament draws to be lop-sided, with the majority of the big names packed into one half of the draw. In these situations it can pay to concentrate on those with strong claims of emerging from the weaker half as usually they will comfortably make the business end and give you the chance to recover your original outlay or close out for a profit before they face the player to progress from the stronger half.

Short-priced tournament favourites have a major influence on the way outright markets evolve. Providing the jolly remains in the tournament and is playing well enough to produce his best tennis, the prices of his rivals in the same half of the draw are unlikely to dramatically shorten as the tournament moves towards its completion courtesy of the fact that they will have to face the favourite at some stage before the final.

Consequently, when looking to back big-priced outsiders in tournaments of this type it's a wise move to concentrate solely on the other half of the draw. ▓

ignore percieved wisdom for cricket gains

HIT RIVALS FOR SIX

ONCE UPON A TIME, AND NOT SO many years ago, cricket betting was, for most serious punters, one of the most moribund areas of sports betting you could find.

By JOHN IZE

Spread betting provided an exciting if high-risk option but for fixed-odds punters the number of markets was limited with match odds and top-scorer the usual fare and when it came to in-running betting, well you could simply forget about it in any competitive sense.

Then betting exchanges came along and split the betting atom. Finally here was a chance for punters to take their skills firmly into the real world – rather than the margin-choked domain of the friendly bookie – and to exploit the eighth wonder of the world that is in-running betting.

Inevitably though, as is the case with most of the betting-friendly sports, the opportunities provided by the introduction of the betting exchanges has over time also seen the sophistication levels of most punters increasing.

This means that profits, at times at least, can be harder to find than used to be the case.

However, cricket is a game of such complexity and with so many variables that the prepared punter will almost certainly be a winning one.

WHO GIVES A TOSS? That cricket allows us to bet on the toss of a coin is a nice simple way to start trading a game. More appealing is the fact that quite often you're able to get away with laying bets on the exchanges which, in gambling terms, are the ultimate in mug bets.

Anyone who has ever repeatedly tossed a coin will know that, despite the ratio of heads and tails falling close to 50:50, as you continue to toss there will be times in the sequence of spins when one side of the coin will repeatedly turn up for a number of throws.

This isn't because there's anything necessarily wrong with the coin or the throw, but time and again in cricket we hear of one captain or another consistently losing the toss and the reasons behind this are generally described in terms that are in actual fact little short of superstitious nonsense.

When this happens, and unbelievably such hocus-pocus rears its head on a semiregular basis, it has been possible for punters to create for themselves the dream bet whereby they can lay someone winning the toss at a shorter price than the even money punt it should be.

Aside from the ludicrous bets that one can make on the toss, there is also the small matter of the effect winning the toss can have on the actual result of the game.

This particular aspect of the coin-spin should be of interest to cricket punters given that there are two directly opposing schools of thought with regard to the effect of winning the toss.

Cricket punters appear to love nothing more than to over-react at certain points in a game and the toss is one of them. On the face of it the side that wins and thus gets to decide whether the conditions are

On Betfair you can even bet on the outcome of the toss

ripe for bowlers or batsmen would appear to be in a significantly stronger position than their opponents.

In day/night games the effect would seem to be even greater still.

However, there is a considerable body of evidence which says that, contrary to the general perception, winning the toss has very little effect on the eventual result in the one-day game and none whatsoever in first class games of three or more days.

Much of this work has been carried out by Australian statisticians, all of whom appear to have independently arrived at this same broad conclusion, the implications of which are huge for punters looking to profit from small, but nevertheless, incorrect movements in the market.

All have found that by using basic statistical tests on the results of winners of the toss and the eventual game winners that there is absolutely no evidence to say that the winning of the toss has any real effect on the result.

There's no doubting that this turns

become a
weather man

rain leads to overreaction

All Test matches use five-day forecasts in order to attempt to calculate how many hours will be lost during play to the weather. Too often the threat of rain, particularly in England, can be over-played with the consequence that the draw price is frequently shorter than it should be, particularly with the historic trend for Test matches becoming shorter.

conventional thinking on its head, but until such a time that cricket fans can explain why the solid mathematical evidence is contrary to their interpretations the judgement of the number-crunchers should be trusted over those of the barmy army.

WEATHER Cricket's relationship with the weather is well-known and an understanding of what the local conditions for a game can mean in terms of the eventual result is essential if you're to trade successfully.

Aside from the actual strength of the teams involved there is probably no more important factor in any single game, whether Test or ODI, than the prevailing weather conditions.

For one-day games there's no difficulty in taking hour-by-hour forecasts for the ground in question and looking not just for obvious things like rain but also for possible changes in humidity over the course of the day.

FORECASTING RUNS Perhaps the biggest red herring that gets thrown the way of cricket fans and punters alike is when people start talking of predictions in terms of run-rates during a one-day game.

Television companies are by far and away the worst perpetrators in endless quoting of almost-meaningless run-rate projections, although as providers of entertainment we can't necessarily blame them for using them to fill in the gaps between balls.

Instead, it's up to the shrewd cricket punter to punish anyone who places too much store in using run-rates to calculate match results.

There is no reason why a punter should ever suppose that because a team has scored an average of four and a half runs per over in the previous 25 overs why they'll go on and score at exactly the same rate in the subsequent 25 given that the composition of both the bowlers and the batsmen will differ.

Another way to approach forecasting a team's final total of runs is by using a system such as Duckworth Lewis. However, with a complexity level that is little short of quantum mechanics, most punters will only encounter it when the heavens open and the statisticians try to work out how to adjust the number of runs and overs in line with the amount of interruption there has been to the game.

With its complexity has come a degree of cynicism towards the method, which in turn has only helped the significant number of professional punters and syndicates that use the method or others based on its ideas.

The reason for this is that behind the complex mathematics that are used to solve the problem of weather-interrupted games is a method that at times lends itself with stunning accuracy to forecasting the eventual total for a side's innings.

Without going into the intricacies of the Duckworth Lewis method it shouldn't complicate things to say that the system works by assessing each side's innings in terms of a set of remaining resources, namely the balls left to be faced and the number of wickets they have remaining.

As each ball is bowled or wicket is taken the resources available to the batting side diminishes, as does the number of runs that they're expected to score by the end of the innings.

While on paper the Duckworth Lewis method looks to be a really useful betting tool, the reality is that in its original form there are some fundamental problems.

Aside from the prohibitively complex mathematics that power its forecasts, another big criticism that is levelled at it is that it initially calculates its run forecasts from an overall average figure.

This means that before a ball is bowled both sides are rated at the same strength with no modification to allow for what can be in effect big differences.

So whether it's Australia versus Bangladesh at the MCG or England meeting Scotland at Lord's each side, in the Duckworth Lewis world, starts the game as an even money shot.

Despite this considerable drawback, when you need a forecast during the second innings of a closely-fought game between two sides of comparable ability Duckworth Lewis more often that not comes up trumps in a way that simple calculations of run-rate based forecasts simply cannot match.

STATS Luckily for cricket punters the sport's long tradition of accurate record-keeping means that we're spoilt for choice when it comes to finding stats to research any aspect of the game.

Whether it be pertaining to the ground, match type, the overall record of the teams involved or breaking it down further into each player's individual batting and bowling records, there are more than enough stats to point the way to profit providing you take the time to go through them with a fine-tooth comb.

None of these records should assume more importance than the other, with a decent study of each providing a more than solid basis for which to go on and forecast a game.

The internet has proved a boon for cricket punters with a wealth of information available from established sites such as www.cricinfo.com, or my own personal favourite www.howstat.com.au.

Ground and historic records are without question the first port of call and an important one at that. You'll get nowhere if, prior to looking at player and team statistics, you don't determine what sort of wicket they're playing on as well as the historic scoring and wicket trends for the ground.

There are a multitude of ways of approaching team and player statistics, ranging from simple averaging of scores at the bottom end to complex mathematical forecasts at the cutting edge.

One of the more obscure areas of cricket analysis comes from the stat-heavy world of baseball in the shape of Sabermetrics.

Most punters will know how much the Yanks love keeping a variety of sports stats ranging from the general to the completely obscure.

Having been greeted with a significant degree of derision when they first appeared in the US back in the 1970s, Sabermetric have over the past 30 years gradually received a great deal of acceptance from NBL teams as well as professional punters and bookmakers.

Sabermetrics are designed to take general statistics such as, in a cricketing context, batting and bowling averages one step further on with the specific intention of using them to objectively measure the worth of each player's contribution as well as those for the strength of his team.

While that might sound complicated, in reality they are very simple but in their simplicity lies some sound theory and potentially profitable ways of looking at player statistics.

MORE RUNS = MORE WICKETS

Finally, it's as true for cricket as it is with many other sports that the harder a team push forward the more likelihood there is for disaster to befall them. It's not difficult to see how a football team, a goal behind in the late stages of a game and throwing players forward in search of an equaliser, can be caught on the counter-attack by their opponents, and it's no less true of cricket.

A team pushing beyond the limit of their

usual scoring rate lose more wickets as a consequence of doing so.

In short if you take more chances then you increase the risk of something negative happening.

We see this occurring frequently in the one-day game where a team will suddenly increase their current rate of scoring and, with the assumption that the batsmen have 'played themselves in', their team's price in the market contracts accordingly.

In such situations it's usually the case that the side that is batting becomes too short in the market.

Add a few spectacular boundaries into the mix to shorten the price even further and the whole thing, more often than not, becomes a layers' paradise as the consequence of all that run-making as often as not results in a steady trickle of wickets and the batting team ends its innings having never fared quite as well as their short-term run-rate suggested.

Of course there'll be times when having 'played themselves in' that one of the men at the crease will stay and build a decent total for his team but more often that not it doesn't happen.

Finally, if you don't want to work too hard, employ one betting strategy for Tests in England – simply lay the draw.

It's now a well-established fact that bettors on the sub-continent plunge on the draw at lower odds than are available in England, leaving their layers to hedge on Betfair.

That forces the prices down to below what they should be, so you are invariably getting decent value.

Some day the market will correct itself, but as long a the draw price remains artificially low, it would be rude not to get involved. ■

finding the edge in your chosen discipline

GENERAL SPORTS

New England face Philadelphia in the 2005 Super Bowl

NFL

By PHIL AGIUS,
BRUCE
MILLINGTON
& PAUL KEALY

THE stop-start nature of American football matches makes them ideal for in-running trading on the exchanges, *writes Phil Agius*.

For example, the 2005 Super Bowl between New England and Philadelphia was broken up into 169 total plays, bite-sized segments after each of which a punter might have wanted to change his position on the match outcome, total points or handicap line.

With breaks for injuries, time-outs (up to six per half) plus half-time and the end of the first and third quarters, there are ample opportunities for those who want to trade the game, or who suddenly decide they want to take a mighty position on one of the outcomes based on what they have seen to that point.

Odds will invariably open somewhere near the prevailing fixed-odds prices for the match, but those who wait until near gametime for their bets will have far more information at their fingertips and can gain an edge by getting involved early.

For example, the NFL's injury information is among the best in the world – teams supply the league with official updates throughout the week rating players' chances of making the line-up. But it is not until 30 minutes before the game that every member of a team's roster must be declared active or inactive for that match.

Except for major play-off matches, the only reliable sources of this information are the major US websites such as espn.com and cnnsi.com. Finding out from those which playing who were rated questionable starters will actually be on the field and which expected starters have surprisingly been scratched can give the match prices a very different look.

And for televised matches, make sure you get a good look at the pitch and weather conditions as soon as the pre-match cameras go over to the stadium for the first time. The presence of unexpected standing water or the absence of expected snow can have a major effect on both the points total and which team the conditions are likely to suit. Get on early and you'll be well placed to lock in a profit when less clued-up punters latch on to the situation.

The early minutes of the game should also tell you much about whether the pre-match analysis was on the money or not. Various pundits may have been screaming all week that Team A's defensive line will pound Team B's quarterback into submission, but if he's completed six out of eight passes without being sacked as the end of the first quarter approaches, the likelihood is that Team A's head coach has some thinking to do and that Team B, whose offensive line are performing better than billed, may have been a value price at the outset and could still be one – then again, an over-reaction could have occured.

The 1.01 club often seem taken by surprise at comebacks in other sports but they should be even more wary in NFL games.

A team's match odds will no doubt shorten as they approach their opponents' endzone, and the likelihood of an imminent seven points will certainly begin to factor into their price as they get inside the ten-yard line.

But bear in mind that an interception returned the distance for a touchdown the other way could quickly bring about a 14-point swing from the match situation that looked likely. Turnovers (lost fumbles and interceptions) are killers for those who assume too much in NFL betting and they happen far too often for comfort.

Yet as an in-running exchange punter you can set the trap for those too eager to accept that everything will go according to the offence's plan. Remember, you get to set the odds, and you can always price the match up as though the expected touch-down has been recorded. And you will be amazed at how many times you will see someone take your price only to see a breakdown in play.

There's no major edge to be gained from following the game live on the internet while simultaneously watching it on TV and trading, as the timelag on the internet scoring sites (nfl.com, espn and cnnsi as above) seems to be approximately the

beware NFL replacements

 injuries can be crucial

Injuries that occur during the match can often be overreacted to in-running, but don't be dogmatic about backing the team that loses a player – if a concussed quarterback is to be replaced by a starry-eyed rookie back-up, that team could be in real trouble.

When betting on match handicaps in running (Betfair regularly offer at least three lines on each game, e.g. Detroit –3.5pts, -7.5pts and –11.5pts), always remember that margin of victory is unimportant to NFL teams. All punters on the sport have been left screaming at TV screens at some point as the team they need to win by ten points happily let the clock run out as they have the ball on their opponents' three-yard line.

same as the satellite TV coverage. However, those determined to get the news first may get some value from signing up for live internet radio broadcasts, which can be a couple of seconds ahead of the TV coverage. The local radio stations of each team often have live and free streaming and addresses can be discovered reasonably easily on the internet.

FORMULA ONE

CHANGES to both the qualifying format and the technical regulations mean that pinning down a successful in-running strategy in Formula One betting is like trying to hit a moving target, *writes Phil Agius*.

However, as with all sports, the more information you have the better equipped you will be to stay one step ahead of your fellow exchange punters after the starting lights go out.

And you can put your knowledge to good use from the start. Under current regulations, computer software that controls cars' clutch and traction away from the line can mean far more than human talent in the race to the first corner and teams who make consistently good starts are well worth backing at the outset.

For example, in 2004 and 2005 Renault was the class of the field away from the line, regularly making up several places on the first lap due to their excellent gadgetry, while Williams often wasted good grid positions by pulling away like pregnant walruses. Regularly backing-to-lay the Renaults would have produced an excellent return.

Also bear in mind the fuel loads teams are carrying at the start – those who were carrying less fuel in qualifying (cars must be filled with the load with which they intend to start the race) will find it easier to get away than those bloated on petrol for a longer first stint. Working out which cars they are (because race tactics are a

Using the internet can be the best way to keep track of F1 race news

matter of utmost secrecy on the Friday and Saturday of grand prix meetings) will come with experience. The best policy is to monitor teams' performances throughout the free practice sessions. If a team have posted the fastest times in three of the four practices, but are a little off the pace without having made any noticeable mistakes on their qualifying laps, there is every reason to expect them to be planning one fewer fuel stop in the race (teams can no longer change tyres at pit-stops under 2005 regulations).

So unless there is a reason why conditions may not longer suit that team's set-up, backing the practice flyers early on, expecting to reap the benefits as the pit-stops unravel in the race itself, can often pay off.

Listening to the TV commentators is valuable, not only for when they make a pertinent point, but also because many of your rival punters will think they have made one when in fact they have boobed.

For example, if you hear the man on the box mistakenly say that second-placed

Kimi Raikkonen has emerged ahead of leader Fernando Alonso after the second pit-stop, when you know that the TV pictures are in fact showing their respective team-mates Juan Pablo Montoya and Giancarlo Fisichella rejoining in fifth and sixth, get cracking. It happens and people do fall for it. A more subtle way of benefiting from in-depth knowledge is to make sure you never trade a race without having the live computer timing from the track on your computer screen too.

The service is available free, although you must register, from the sport's official website www.formula1.com and is an invaluable weapon. It gives punters exactly the same information that the team bosses in the pitlane have on the race, showing the overall standings, lap and sector times, track conditions and highlighting which drivers have just set personal or race-best lap times.

That means that regardless of what is being shown to TV viewers worldwide, probably no more than three or four cars at a time, you know precisely what the whole field is up to. Comparing drivers' lap times shows which ones are likely to be making moves up and down the standings in the near future (allowing you to pre-empt price movements).

And, crucially, you will also be clued-up as to what is going on when TV hosts go to their infuriating advertising breaks. Anyone who had backed Alonso or laid Michael Schumacher must have had itchy fingers on their keyboards when ITV idiotically went to adverts with four laps remaining in the 2005 San Marino Grand Prix with a charging Schumi right on the tail of the Spaniard, whose tyres were shot.

However, those with the timing in front of them knew that Alonso was making his car big in every corner and keeping the German behind him while TV-only punters sweated it out until ITV deigned to return for the last lap.

169

GREYHOUND RACING

I never thought I'd see the day when I was dishing out advice on how to make money out of greyhound racing, *writes Paul Kealy*.

I know little more about greyhounds than I do your common mongrel (four legs, a head, tail etc), but the good news is that I don't need to as greyhounds, particularly BAGS racing, can be a licence to print money for traders and there is no need to study form or even watch the things.

It is pretty much accepted that afternoon dog racing is no more than a numbers game designed to fleece betting shop punters. It is usually low class, the races tend to be tightly graded and the bookmakers' percentages are quite disgraceful.

It is not unknown to see all six dogs in a race open up at 3-1, giving a book of 150 per cent – some 48 per cent (or more) higher than you will see on an exchange.

Yet because this is such a mugs' game, there is very, very little serious money going around. Just pay a visit to your local afternoon dog meeting. I once went to Crayford on a bitterly cold day. In attendance were three bookmakers offering prices from the bar, me, a mate, two old men, some bookies' representatives and the barmaid.

There is next to no on-course betting, and very little office money (to shorten up runners by bookmakers) unless there is a perceived track bias giving an advantage to either inside or outside runners as plenty of betting shop mugs like to do forecast multiples.

So unlike in horse racing, where the Betfair market is basically a mirror image of the on-course market (some would say the other way round nowadays) albeit with better prices, the greyhound market is not monitored anywhere near as closely by the major bookmakers because potential liabilities are always much smaller.

Watch a horse shorten up on Betfair and

you can be 100 per cent certain that its price will contract on course and in the betting shops as well. But that doesn't happen in BAGS racing.

Given the massive percentages that bookies work to, you would expect every hound on Betfair to be offered at much-inflated prices. Not so.

Yes, you can often get 10-1 about a 3-1 chance and 20-1 about an 8-1 chance, but in several races a day there will be so much money centred about one dog that its price collapses and it ends up a good deal shorter than you can back it at with Messrs Coral, Hills, Ladbrokes et al.

This is what is known as trading heaven. It's free money.

There are various theories as to why this happens. A lot of these occurrences tend to happen in midwinter after the day's horse racing action has finished, which strongly suggests a lot of people are throw-

explaining the greyhound plunges

 shrewdies will take a price as long as value exists

My colleagues on the greyhound desk at the Racing Post have an explanation for the disparity in BAGS greyhound prices on Betfair.

While they acknowledge that on-course layers are under instructions to bet to tight percentages, they suggest that often the prices about the outsiders are far too short, while the serious contenders are too big. Remember, on-course layers can price dogs up any way they wish because they are taking very little money.

So what arrives on Betfair is money from shrewd greyhound punters who have long been closed down by the major bookies. And they will accept below the current betting shop show as long as the price they are getting is considered to be bigger than its genuine chance of winning. They are still getting

a value bet and are happy to play.

That sounds a bit far-fetched, but at least one of our greyhound boys has been prohibited from betting on dogs with one of the Big Three bookmakers.

How much is down solely to his ability as a dog judge we can only guess at, though, and in any case it would be irresponsible to advise in a book about value punting on betting exchanges that you simply lump on the best-backed dogs throughout the afternoon.

I spent a couple of days religiously following the greyhound betting movements and backing those shorter on Betfair with the bookies.

The result was a very small profit, although it would have been bigger if I had simply traded on every one. It's still a too-small sample to be dogmatic about, though.

ing away money through boredom betting on those cold afternoons.

But whatever the true reason, the phenomenon of dogs being available to lay at shorter prices than you can back in a betting shop or on the internet definitely exists and you can make money by either laying the dogs on Betfair and backing them to the same stake with your bookie to guarantee a free bet, or having a bit less on with your bookie to guarantee a win whatever happens.

For instance, you could lay £250 at 3 (2-1) on Betfair and have £187 at 3-1 with Hills. You win £60 quid after five per cent commission if it loses and also win £61 if it wins. That's a simple example, and sometimes the price discrepancies aren't that big – believe it or not, sometimes they are bigger – but because the major bookmakers pay little or no attention to the exchange market on greyhounds you are under no time pressure to get your bets on.

How long this phenomenon will last is anyone's guess, but for well over a year punters have been able to play the bookies off against the exchanges for no risk at all.

Long may it continue.

BOXING

The fight game has a long way to go to capture the imagination of in-running punters judging by the relatively light betting that goes on during most televised bouts, *writes Paul Kealy*.

That can largely be put down to the fact that most of the action we get to see in the UK is of one-sided contests with dubious betting appeal from the outset, while all the big contests tend to take place in Las Vegas and thus in the early hours of the morning UK time.

However, there are occasionally some high-profile fights that attract plenty of in-running cash and there is money to be made if you know what to look out for.

Sky Sports' Jim Watt (right) is the ultimate perfectionist

I've long been an advocate of watching live sport with the sound turned down, largely because the commentators can put thoughts into your head that you may not have originally shared (see *Let Your Eyes Guide You*, chapter 18) and if you know your sport you should not need telling what is going on.

However, commentators can, and often do, affect the market and this can work in your favour if you disagree (and happen to be right).

Most of the fights you will see are shown on Sky (although ITV made a welcome return in July 2005), so here is my idea of what you should expect from their two most-used commentators.

Ian Darke: Could probably do with a shot or two of valium before going on air as he often appears a shade excited. Admittedly, this is probably by design as it's his job to build up the viewers' excitement levels and this he does very well.

He also appears all too eager to be dazzled by the big-name fighter and some-

make use of those body shots

**when appearances
can affect the market**

Understanding body language is not something that everyone can become an expert at, but on the night in 2005 that Ricky Hatton challenged light-welterweight legend Kostya Tszyu it seemed the world and his wife could read the Hitman's manager, Frank Warren, like a book.

Walking towards the ring and once inside it, Warren looked like a man who knew he was about to lose the goose that laid the golden egg. Fear was written all over his face, and whatever he may say afterwards, it seemd pretty obvious to viewers that did not expect to be hailing Hatton as the new IBF champion.

Many fight fans on the Betfair chatroom made the same observations, and all the talk was of Hatton's impending doom against the Thunder From Down Under.

At the same time Hatton did not look remotely on edge – if anything he looked more determined than ever – but Warren's appearance was enough to start a dramatic pre-fight drift. Hatton was a top-priced 9-4 chance on the day of the fight, but bookmakers were reporting a wholesale gamble on the Manchester man, who was down to 5-4 with some firms according to Sky.

Not on Betfair, though. As the clock ticked away to the opening bell, Hatton almost touched 3-1, all on the back of a petrified-looking manager.

times tends to ignore the less spectacular but possibly more effective work of the underdog. This can be good news because a hot favourite can end up even shorter in-running despite the fact that the contest could be becoming very tight. Darke is very forthright, often to the point of being absolutely certain of the result even if his own card has one boxer only two points ahead.

Jim Watt: No-one knows his boxing like the Scot but he can have the opposite effect on the favourite's price because he is such a perfectionist. You have to put up a virtually flawless performance to impress Watt during a fight as he spots every wrong move. Watt is more often than not right about his assessment of the action but it doesn't necessarily mean that the man he is criticising is losing. Quite often he is winning, just not as well as Watt would like him to be.

Other things to look out for are pretty

straightforward. Make sure you know where the judges originate from, as it is well known that Americans favour an aggressive style. Also, if you are going to be cynical about the fight game – and a lot of the time it's hard not to be – make sure you apply that cynicism at all venues.

It seems to be generally accepted in the UK that it is very hard for a British fighter to travel to Europe – Germany and Italy are particularly singled out – and earn a points decision.

It's possibly true given some of the bad decisions over the years, but it is equally true of Britain, where there have also been some dreadful home verdicts over the years. We just tend not to make such a fuss of them.

And of course, any section on boxing betting has to come with a serious wealth warning. No matter how right you feel you have called it, be prepared to lose as shocking judging – whether by accident or design – has always plagued the sport.

CYCLING

IN the ever-widening world of exchange betting, cycling remains small beer, but for three weeks every summer it provides an oasis for those who have an opinion on the sport and want to put their spoke in with hard cash, *writes Bruce Millington*.

Betfair provides a unique playground for Tour de France punters whose problem before it came into existence was finding ways to get on.

Traditional bookmakers and spread firms have both found cycling a costly sport to bet on. It is simply impossible to justify the employment of a full-time cycling expert – it would make no economic sense and he would spend much of his year finding ways of filling his working day – so firms tend to rely on their most knowledgeable staff member to try to provide a service that doesn't turn out to be disastrously expensive. And though these guys are usually extremely bright and capable, they are always vulnerable to punters who are close to the action and can pick off their bad prices at will.

The upshot has been a general reticence to offer much beyond the basic outright and stage markets, which are traded to high percentages and small volumes.

Thankfully, help is at hand thanks to Betfair, where you will, of course, suffer no such thing as a knockback. And nor will you find daily stage markets suspended the moment the riders start pedalling, even though they invariably have scores of kilometres to cover before any meaningful action takes place.

Because Betfair doesn't care who wins or loses, you can bet on a stage right until the second before they cross the line.

Mountain stages are a spectacular betting medium, as prices flicker with each grimace or surge by the riders hauling themselves up brutally steep roads.

And long-term markets offer a good chance to trade in and out of positions and also to make a quick buck as wise owls monitor them as key stages are taking place.

One slight problem can be a lack of liquidity. You may have a hunch for an outsider only to find he is priced up fairly conservatively. But, in adherence with the general rule on exchanges, don't be afraid to ask for a fancy price.

In the 2005 Tour I fancied a little-known Spaniard for a particular stage. The best price to back him, as with a number of those at the bottom of the list, was 50 but I requested £10 at 400 and had £7 matched. If you don't ask, you don't get. ■

the clear choice for novelty bets

ALWAYS OPEN FOR TRADE

By BRUCE MILLINGTON

YOU COULD SPEND ALL DAY making a list of the great things about betting exchanges and still overlook some fundamental advantages.

Bookmakers would doubtless try to counter most of the points on your list but one area of betting which they would have absolutely no right to dispute concerns novelty markets, where it is nigh-on impossible to even begin trying to claim a traditional bookmaker can offer a better service than an exchange (actually, let's cut to the chase and refer specifically to Betfair rather than 'exchanges' as if there are dozens of comparable products).

I suppose everyone who backed Denmark at 66-1 with William Hill to win the 2000 Eurovision Song Contest when, the eventual winners having finished their performance to rapturous applause which the Hills compiler clearly missed, 6-1 was the general price elsewhere would argue that you do not have to put your novelty business the way of Betfair to land a touch.

And nor would those people who want an individual price based on them losing 15 stone by Christmas or on their newborn child to play for England. They know that Graham Sharpe of Hills is the man to see for a tailored service of that nature.

But for anyone else who wants to get stuck into a reality TV show, snow to fall on Christmas Day, the identity of the next Pope or the next Liverpool manager, Betfair should be the first port of call. It will usually be the last as well.

And the reason these more outlandish markets and Betfair were made for each other? Simple. Traditional bookmakers, perfectly understandably, do not want to risk losing large sums on events which, to a greater or lesser degree, are less trustworthy and more volatile than, say, the 2.30 at Newmarket or the Merseyside derby.

Take Big Brother, which epitomises why a punter who takes his business to anyone bar Betfair is not doing his wallet any favours.

Here is the situation. A dozen assorted crazy fame-seekers are locked in a house for the summer, during which time they row, fight, fornicate, backstab and – occasionally – make friends with each other. Once a week one of them is voted out by a combination of themselves and the public until there is a winner.

Walk into any high street betting shop and you will be able to bet on who that winner will be, who will be the longest-lasting male and female, the winner's gender and who the next evictee will be.

As long as your fistful of notes does not contain too many notes, that is. Wander to the counter and ask for two grand on Zelda, or whoever, and you will almost certainly get a knockback. It's not hard to work out why. If you were a bookie and someone you had never seen before wanted a lumpy bet on some unhinged gothic bisexual to outlast a similarly peculiar bunch of people you would smell a rat.

You would probably think that to be risking that kind of sum you must either work for the company that produces the programme or know someone who does. Let's face it, the various phone votes that are conducted during the course of Big Brother must give those privy to the figures they throw up a fairly clear indication of where the Great British public's affection lies.

And given that BB is an entertainment show whose purpose is to boost ratings and thus maximise advertising revenues rather than a sporting event run primarily for the stimulation of betting turnover, those who may choose to use their inside knowledge to nick a few quid are not breaking the rules of a particular licence and are, at worst, operating unethically rather than illegally.

The point is, if they take their business to Betfair and find someone willing to lay their two grand on Zelda, Betfair itself is more than happy to act as the conduit that makes it happen.

In other words, if someone has inside info of any sort (although this doesn't apply to mainstream sports, where the company is conscious of its responsibility not to provide a platform for the corrupt to prosper) they are welcome at Betfair.

When it comes to novelty markets, Betfair is no place for the faint-hearted. You may leave an order up to back a Mariah Carey soundalike to win 'Stars In Their Eyes' only to find it matched by a member of the dance troupe who are supporting her who has heard her struggle through rehearsals because she has chronic stage-fright and laryngitis.

When this croaking, nervous wreck shuffles on to the stage and opens her mouth, and the sheer hopelessness of her chances becomes apparent, there is no point those who backed her crying about it.

And if it is not someone in the know legging you over, there are the rampers to watch out for. These cunning rats populate the Betfair forum and will think nothing of putting away their fellow users by dropping in a plausible-sounding but totally false post.

A classic example of this came in the 2005 Big Brother, when two characters called Science and Maxwell were involved in an eviction head-to-head. There had been a perceived undercurrent of racial tension throughout the show and a thread on the forum appeared from someone claiming to be watching the live feed (the majority of Big Brother viewers take in only the nightly highlights shows which cover the previous day), who stated that Maxwell, who is white, had called Science, who is black, a particularly repellent racial insult.

This was utterly untrue (and yet another example of Betfair taking a huge risk by tolerating postings that sail so close to the wind from a legal perspective), but it did not prevent a flurry of activity on the next eviction market as a number of people swallowed the bait and laid Maxwell on the premise that he was bound to have disgusted the voting public and was consequently destined to be evicted.

Taking away all forms of shenanigans and skulduggery, though, from the blatant misuse of sensitive information to the ingenious ramp, novelty markets work so well on Betfair because, as with all forms of betting on the exchange, there is tremendous value, ample trading opportunities, a wide range of markets and almost constant accessibility.

Indeed I have spoken to a number of figures in the betting industry who freely admit that Betfair makes their life easy where things like Big Brother are concerned

punting on the papacy

 vatican value

While Paddy Power were mopping up on the publicity stakes by touting their next Pope market in the spring of 2005, Betfair was the focal point for those who had a view on John Paul II's successor.

There was frantic activity when the black smoke first wafted above the Vatican to announce that the conclave had chosen their man. In the 20 minutes between that eagerly-awaited signal and the emergence of the winner, Cardinal Joseph Ratzinger, some sharp minds tried the old trick of forcing the price of randomly chosen outsiders from around 400 right down to 4 – the lack of liquidity meant this could be done for less than £30 – and then putting up a meaty order to lay at, say, 6 in the hope of hooking panic backers who saw the price collapse and thought they were jumping on the successful bandwagon.

In the event, Ratzinger was always among the favourites.

because they can use the current exchange prices as a tissue and simply trim the percentages so that they can offer a service to their non-exchange-literate customers.

And when these firms want to close their book, limit bet sizes or whatever it takes to prevent them being hoodwinked or stung they can do so with ease.

Betfair knows that novelty betting is not a core part of its plan for global betting domination, but it also knows that it is an important vehicle both for publicity and for stimulating growth in areas where other more cautious betting companies would never dare to tread with any purpose.

ALWAYS READ THE GREY TEXT

The grey text is the name given to the wording that appears when you click on the rules section that appears to the right of each market interface.

For most sports this is standard text which is virtually self-explanatory.

For specials and novelties it is important that anyone placing a bet digests the grey text before getting involved. Because of the unpredictability of some more obscure Betfair markets, you need to be aware of what might happen to your bet if, as happens from time to time, unforeseen circumstances arise.

This is especially the case where Big Brother is concerned, and there have been two delicate situations arising from controversial evictions.

In the 2004 version, a housemate was hurriedly ejected from the show for allegedly pulling a knife on a fellow contestant. This caused a problem because some punters thought they were betting on the next scheduled eviction and others on which housemate would be the next to leave the house.

And in 2005 the standard eviction procedure was altered one week so that of the six nominated housemates, the two that received the most votes from the public were made known to the other seven remaining hopefuls, who then had to choose which one was chucked out.

Betfair had covered themselves by saying that the market would be voided if the next evictee was chosen by any other means than a public vote. ■

keeping a clear head
AVOID THE PITFALLS

ALWAYS CHECK THE BET YOU

By PAUL KEALY

requested is correct. This seems blindingly obvious, but we ought to start with simplicity and in any case many a disastrous trade has been struck by punters clicking on the wrong button.

Betting in-running is a real pressure-charged pursuit in which reaction time can be all important. Too much hesitation will see you miss a price. However, too much haste can be even more costly. Almost everyone has a tale to tell about pressing the wrong button and I have certainly done it far too many times for comfort myself, but my favourite concerns a colleague at the *Racing Post*.

In a women's tennis match at Wimbledon, he took the view that Daniela Hantuchova was a terrific lay at long odds-on against Shinobu Asagoe because she was known to have a fragile temperament, while much of the nation's press had been on her back following her dramatic weight loss. Having won the first seven games, Hantuchova was being piled into at 1.02 and my colleague, who shall remain nameless, decided it was time to step in.

Unfortunately, however, he hit back instead of lay, so from his intention of risking a few quid to win a few hundred, he had actually risked a few hundred for

Daniel Hantuchova was beaten at odds of 1.02 at Wimbledon

peanuts. And you know what's coming next. Asagoe forced her way into the game, won the second set 6-4, and the 104-minute third 12-10. Ouch.

MAKE SURE YOU ARE AWARE OF THE RULES Another plainly obvious piece of advice you may think, but many of the rules on Betfair are not what you will find elsewhere in the betting industry.

Place betting on horses is a good example. If there is a non-runner in a 16-runner race all bookmakers will reduce the place terms to a quarter the first three rather than first four. On Betfair you will still be be backing or laying for four places as their place terms stick rigidly to the number of declared runners.

I found that out to my cost early in 2001 when laying a horse to be placed in a 14-runner race. It finished fourth, but because there were two non-runners (which I knew about before I placed the bet) and therefore 16 declared, my bet was a loser. Complaints that Betfair's rule was out of synch with the

uncommon knowledge

beware falling foul of unusual ante post rules

Some of Betfair's ante post rules can be described as strange, not least the non-runner no bet rule. For all ante-post horseracing, any bets on non-runners are considered losers, as is normal bookmaking practice. However, the same cannot be said for all sports. Once the draw has been made for a tennis event most bookmakers will adopt a non-runner no bet stance, but before that all bets come under usual long-term rules. On Betfair, however, all bets are considered void if the player in question does not appear in the main draw. It is the same in snooker.

There are two ways to look at this, of course. First, it is terrific news for the backer. However, it always seems to catch out the layer. There have been plenty of examples of tennis players drifting out to unrealistic prices on the back of rumours that they may not show up. But if they don't, it's money-back time and if they do turn out, the backer has a great value price. In the case of the 2005 World Championship

snooker, just two weeks before the main event proper started Betfair listed 48 players in their outright market. These were the world's top 16 plus the 32 who were involved in final qualifying. One of those was Stephen Maguire, up to No. 3 in the world after winning the UK Championship in November, but who still had to qualify. He had been backed at as short as 5.9 for world title glory yet was freely on offer at around 11 before his qualifying match with the promising Ryan Day. However, Betfair's rules state that if a player does not appear in the main draw bets are void, so those laying Maguire – and any of the other 15 losers – could only have struck a winning bet if the selections they had laid qualified for Sheffield. I received a few calls of complaint from punters to the *Racing Post* and shared their disbelief at such a rule. Still do. However, any exchange has a right to settle a market in any way they wish provided the rules are clearly displayed, and these were.

rest of the industry and ludicrous to boot fell, quite rightly, on deaf ears. At the end of the day, the rules are clearly flagged up on the website – in what the call the 'grey text' – and it was up to me to be aware of them.

KNOW THE RUNNERS IN ADVANCE Scanning down the list of runners to see exactly which one it is that you have spotted going well in a race is a sure way to the poorhouse. For a start you will have missed all the prices and secondly, in your panic you will run the risk of mixing up the colours. The following story remains one of the funniest exchange tales I have come across.

Most of the computers at *Racing Post* HQ are Apple Macs which, as those of you who use them will know, can be hopeless when it comes to Betfair. There are a few PCs, though, and in the early days of Betfair there was quite some competition for them. Anyway, two young punters had taken their positions about five yards apart for a race at Haydock, with both watching the action intently, fingers at the ready.

When the race was over, both stood up and you could not tell if either had won or lost – until they crossed paths in the middle of the office.

Punter 1: 'Some idiot just laid me £500 at evens that winner in the last 100 yards.'

Punter 2: 'Yeah it was me. I got the wrong horse.'

TAKE THE PRICE YOU WANT I know a punter who rarely, if ever, takes the price on offer even if it exceeds his expectations. He is quite a decent winner, so must be doing something right, but I've lost count of the times he has complained about putting up a request and finding out after his selection had won that he did not get his bet taken.

It is true that if you want to maximise the value you get from exchange betting you will do so by snapping up the best odds possible. But there comes a point where greed gets in the way.

Everyone should have a minimum acceptable price – if you bet regardless of price you will lose in the long run – but everyone should also have a figure in their head which, when reached, forces them to bet rather than be greedy waiting for something bigger.

If you think something is a 5-1 chance and you are being offered 12-1, why ask for 14-1? You may be accommodated, but it is just as likely you will see what you believe to be terrific value disappearing before your eyes.

DON'T FOLLOW THE MONEY
BLINDLY
People who follow others in are known as cliff-jumpers. They regularly take the worst price available and cannot possibly win in the long run. You know the type. They sit in a betting shop and watch a horse shorten first from 10-1 to 8-1, then to 6-1 and finally when it hits the bottom price of around 7-2 they step in. There is no hope for these people and no hope for you if that is your betting MO.

The reason for this is gullibility and a safety-in-numbers mentality. The gullibility stems from our childhoods, as our brains are geared to soak up as much information as possible without questioning the validity of that information.

But most of us remain gullible to a frightening extent in adulthood. It's why billions of pounds a year are spent on alternative medicine (if it worked the medical profession would simply embrace it and call it medicine) and it's why astrologers are feted in national newspapers instead of ridiculed and run out of town. The list of cons perpetrated on gullible human beings is endless as there is always a sap out there willing to fall for them – make sure it isn't you.

Just because a price is shortening, it does not give the gambled-on runner a divine right to win. Remember, an independent 2005 survey showed that punters would win following drifters on Betfair and lose if they jumped on the bandwagon and joined in a plunge.

The safety-in-numbers mentality is simply explained. A 6-4 favourite is a 6-4 favourite because the majority of punters think it is the most likely winner, so the safety-in-numbers punter steps in because all those people can't possibly be wrong. Yet by following the majority view, all you are doing most of the time is securing bad value.

If everyone is betting one way, it is a long odds-on shot that the prices being taken

Ricky Hatton on his way to a short price for BBC Sports Personality of the Year. Unfortunately, not short enough

are artificially short. Oppose the majority view and the chances are you have got a value wager.

DON'T OVERREACT In the heat of punting battle you always run the risk of making a rash decision, whether it is in the market you are following at the time or a related one. None of us is immune and I'll give you my own personal example.

When Ricky Hatton was on the verge of victory over Kostya Tszyu in June 2005 I hastily went to Betfair's Sports Personality of the Year market and backed him at 6, thinking he would soon go down to around 3.5 and I would be able to lay him back for a free bet. So you can imagine my horror when Hatton was freely available at 8-1 with the bookies the following day. As a boxing fan, my admiration for Hatton had gone through the roof and I had lost control.

Rational thinking would have enabled me to consider that boxers rarely win the award (only three have done so since 1970) because the sport is deeply unpopular with

This sounds rather contrary given what has just been said on the previous page.

However, it is not when you think about it. When great value is sitting in front of you, you must act, but that does not mean you should not also make outrageous demands on occasions. In a liquid market, it is virtually impossible to snap up a daft price, but in-running betting opens up all sorts of new opportunities.

It is a source of constant amazement what odds get matched. For instance, in the 2003-04 Championship play-offs, Crystal Palace were backed at 970 and 1000 to be promoted when trailing 2-1 on aggregate in the semi-final against Sunderland. They scored in the 90th minute, won the tie on penalties and eventually went on to beat West Ham in Cardiff to earn a Premiership spot.

What is one man's idea of buying money is another's idea of an unbelievable lay. If you don't ask you don't get.

some people and that the fight was not on BBC. He had a bit of a mountain to climb even if his performance was the best by a British boxer for 20 years. I was never in a position to hedge even to get my money back so had to sit tight or close out for a loss. Actually I backed him again but that may largely be due to the fact that I'd had no sleep and was still full of adrenalin.

There are other examples, most notably a brace for Wayne Rooney against Croatia in Euro 2004 forcing his price down to evens to be the tournament's top goalscorer. He was back out to 4.5 by the following morning.

All bets need to be carefully considered. Think of something in the heat of the moment and the chances are someone else already has. They may not have done, but you have to take into consideration the price on offer first.

NEVER BE AFRAID TO GUARANTEE A NO-LOSE BOOK

All betting is littered with if-onlys, whether it's a late goal scuppering a superb bet or a horse getting pipped on the line. At the very worst consider closing out to cover your stake.

Don't forget, as opposed to spreads, you pay barely any margin for covering your position. Most of Betfair's winners are traders, rather than out-and-out punters.

ALWAYS BE ON THE BALL WHEN MARKETS ARE REOPENED

Football remains the only sport in which exchanges suspend betting when the score changes. They also do so if a penalty is awarded. In these incidences, all unmatched bets are cancelled so the market takes time to reform. And you can occasionally nick some great value positions if you put up some unrealistic prices/requests (but not too unrealistic). Most people would struggle to come up with a true price, and there can be some terrific backs and lays before the professionals help the market to settle.

Personally I would rather see all markets left open until the final whistle and I'm sure there would be many punters prepared to trade in the frantic moments leading up to a penalty. This is unlikely to happen, however, as the exchanges are concerned that liquidity would suffer as not many people would be willing to leave chunks of unguarded money sitting around.

CROSS-REFERENCE DIFFERENT MARKETS You can often look to play off one market against another and maybe collect on both. For example, if you have backed 'any unquoted' (which means either team to score four or more) in Betfair's correct-score list and the score is 3-0, look to lay the winning team in the next goal market. If the other team scores, you have won your money on next goal, but if the winning team subsequently scores you have won twice.

A perfect example of this came in a 2005 Champions League match between Chelsea and Barcelona. Trailing 2-1 from the first leg, Chelsea had raced into a 3-0 lead after just 19 minutes at Stamford Bridge and despite Barcelona having plenty of time to get back into the tie punters only had eyes for the Blues.

Any unquoted was on offer at 20 pre-match and you could lay Chelsea at 2.4 in the next goal market when they were 3-0 up. After Barca had scored in the 27th minute, you could again lay Chelsea at 2.5. Barca scored again in the 38th minute, and again Chelsea could be laid at 2.5. This time they scored, but the point is you can guarantee yourself money and give yourself the chance of copping twice.

DON'T IGNORE BOOKMAKERS You can sometimes play off fixed-odds markets against exchanges as well. For instance in September 2003, Blue Square offered 1-2 about Michael Owen scoring for England against Liechtenstein, while Betfair punters were happy to accept 1.37 about Owen beating the whole Liechtenstein team in a scorers match bet. You could have backed him with Blue Square and laid him on Betfair to guarantee yourself a profit whatever happened and still have the possibility of a win on both markets in the unlikely event that Owen scored and Liechtenstein either matched or beat him. Always, make sure you get your bet on first with the bookmaker, though, as they are highly likely to have limits.

ALWAYS KEEP A KEEN EYE ON OUTRIGHT MARKETS It doesn't matter what sport you are following, whether it is Wimbledon tennis, a snooker or football tournament, there are always nuggets of value to be found on the outright as people overreact to something that is happening within the event.

In the 2005 French Open women's singles, Justin Henin-Hardenne was involved in a marathon last-16 battle with Svetlana Kuznetsova, largely because her intermittent back problems had seemed to have resurfaced at just the wrong time. The Belgian girl was unbeaten on clay throughout the season and started as a red-hot 6-4 favourite for the title.

Yet she faced match point against Kuznetsova, who also had the opportunity to serve for the match, and was subsequently backed at 50 on Betfair's outright market. Few women in the game are as mentally tough as Henin-Hardenne, though, and she staved off the danger, winning the match within minutes. That 50 had soon evaporated and Henin-Hardenne was back to being hot favourite. She went on to win the title without dropping another set. Obviously you have to be brave in such situations as your bet could go up in smoke almost straight away, but if there is an over-

John Terry (right) battles for Chelsea against Barcelona at Stamford Bridge in 2005

reaction in a match market that is likely to mirrored elsewhere so it's always worth staying on the lookout. And when you are backing at big prices, it is surely worth the risk.

DON'T TRUST YOUR TV You will have read this elsewhere in the book, but it can't be rammed home often enough. When you are watching a 'live' sport transmission the chances are what you are watching is not actually live, especially if you are viewing via cable or satellite.

It is well known now among racing fans that SIS offers just about the fastest TV feed on offer – although a couple of Irish punters have told me that their coverage appears to be even faster – while the likes of At The Races and Racing UK are up to three seconds behind. That can be a long time, especially when horses are approaching a fence and there is only a one-second delay on bets being placed in-running on Betfair.

And it is pretty much the same with other

You could have got a free bet by backing and laying Michael Owen

sports, although Betfair tend to operate a five-second delay. Digital TV offers many advantages – even the BBC show more sport live thanks to their interactive services – but anything on a digital platform has a slight time delay, which is bad news for in-running punters.

You can check this yourself by watching something live on terrestrial TV and then switching to the same station on digital. So until terrestrial TV goes by the wayside as it eventually will, there will always be differences. However, when terrestrial goes, that does not mean everyone will be on a level playing field.

If you are watching transmissions from a different country, you can be sure that local TV coverage will be ahead. Betting is a global business and Betfair has thousands of overseas clients.

And there will always be punters at the venue who can bet as it happens. That doesn't always work out, though. I once went to Wentworth for the World Matchplay golf and followed Mike Weir and

Thomas Bjorn in an early-morning match. Bjorn was in the trees in two, while Weir faced a five-footer for birdie. I got straight on the phone to a bookmaker to back Weir, who proceeded to three-putt for a bogey, while Bjorn got up and down for a four.

DEALING WITH DISPUTES The

biggest exchange betting dispute of 2005 undoubtedly concerned Adam Scott's 'victory' in the rain-shortened Nissan Open. Scott prevailed in a play-off with Chad Campbell after only 36 holes of regular play had been possible.

But the tournament caused widespread confusion within the bookmaking industry as it had not completed its full course.

Most layers paid out on Scott, with some refunding backers of all the losers, but Betfair opted to completely void the market. They settled on the 'official winner' and according to the USPGA, Scott's victory was unofficial and would not offer the normal priveleges that go with a US Tour success – a two-year Tour exemption that Scott didn't need anyway as he had won the previous year's Players Championship. The waters were further muddied when it was noted that Scott's prize money was 'official' and counted towards the money list.

The problem for Betfair is that they have both backers and layers to consider, so they have to stick rigidly to their rules. For a start, they could not simply void losing bets as that would be taking money away from the layers.

They could only settle with Scott as the winner if they were completely covered by their rules. However, with the US Tour insisting that Scott's win was not 'official', Betfair were hamstrung by their rules and no amount of whining – and I was one of the whiners – was going to make any difference.

Betfair were convinced that any Scott

uncommon knowledge

when IBAS let us down

The Independent Betting Arbitration Service (IBAS) did not cover itself in glory with their ruling on the Adam Scott affair.

The problem IBAS faced was the fact that several bookmakers – Blue Square, Hills, Skybet, Stan James, Stanley and Totesport – had already paid out on Scott yet their rules stated that bets would be settled on the 'official' winner.

Yet here was Betfair, saying they couldn't pay out because bets were settled on the 'official' winner.

In the end IBAS decided that the bookies acted correctly because their rules stated 'official winner irrespective of the number of holes played', while Betfair also acted correctly because their rules just said official result.

How anyone could consider relevant the words 'irrespective of the number of holes played' when the USPGA were adamant that Scott's win was not official is beyond any sane-thinking punter.

layers would be able to take the case to the Independent Betting Arbitration Service and win. And they were proved right.

Looking back, it is hard to be too critical of the bookmakers for their rules. After all, 'official result' would appear to have all angles covered.

Only in America can you win 'official' money for an 'unofficial' win. ▨

the betting industry panics

BOOKIES GO TO WAR

BETTING EXCHANGES ARE A revolution within a revolution, a rapidly growing occupant of a furiously expanding gambling house who many of the older, bigger occupants would like to evict, or lock up in a cupboard, or possibly murder. The big bookmakers' defence would be 'justifiable homicide,' on the grounds of unbearable irritation – and unfair competition.

By DAVID ASHFORTH

Not so much 'exchanges' as 'exchange,' for Betfair is to betting exchanges what Hoover once was to vacuum cleaners and Sellotape to adhesive tape – so dominant in its market that the company name is synonymous with the product. Betfair accounts for over 90 per cent of exchange business, and attracts over 90 per cent of the attacks launched by the exchanges' critics.

It is ironic that an operation lambasted by bookmakers, and sometimes by the BHB, should be lauded by the wider business community. In 2002 Betfair's founders, Andrew Black and Edward Wray, were named as Ernst and Young Emerging Entrepreneurs of the Year; in 2003, Betfair received the Queen's Award for Enterprise; in 2004, the Confederation of British Industry named Betfair Company of the Year in the growing business category.

Betfair stands in stark cultural contrast

with traditional bookmakers who, despite an impressive recent record of innovation, can seem old-fashioned, hard-nosed, remorselessly dedicated to commercial self-interest, grumpy and grudging.

Betfair also pursues its commercial self-interest but has created a different image, that of an ultra-modern, progressive, open and responsible company, a company that welcomes serious debate and examination. Betfair has answered inquisitors and critics with reasoned arguments and an enthusiasm for working with regulatory authorities that has certainly influenced the Jockey Club's attitude, and that of the government.

Visitors to Betfair's modern offices in Hammersmith can hardly avoid being impressed – by the youthful enthusiasm, the confident vigour, the developing technology, the commercial vibrancy. This is the kind of new enterprise that the government wanted to encourage when, in October 2001, it took the revolutionary step of abolishing betting duty and replacing it with a gross profits tax. With a major reform of gambling legislation under way, the government looked forward to a world in which Britain's well regulated gambling industry would serve the world. The switch to GPT paved the way for high-turnover, low-margin products.

Exchange betting is one example but it is not the most successful example, for Betfair is small beer compared to fixed odds betting terminals (machines which allow punters to bet on casino-style games). It is interesting to compare the position of betting exchanges and FOBTs.

In 2003/4, about £2.7 billion was bet on exchanges while Ladbrokes' FOBTs alone attracted over £5 billion. Betfair's total gross profit that year was £49 million, while Ladbrokes' gross profit on FOBTs was about £160 million.

Yet, in the public arena, little was heard

Hills chief executive David Harding is unhappy with profit margins

of FOBTs, which raise serious questions about problem gambling and reduce levy income by diverting business to non-racing products, while a great deal was heard of exchanges.

Bookmakers do not want FOBTs to attract further government attention but they do want attention paid to betting exchanges. They want them shackled. The fundamental reason is the obvious one – betting exchanges pose a threat to the big bookmakers' profitability and market dominance.

For most of the 45 years since betting shops were legalised, the betting business has been dominated by a handful of big suppliers, notably Ladbrokes, William Hill and Coral. The outlets that really mattered were the betting shops, where competition was severely limited. The licensing system made entry into the market difficult, pool betting offered little competition to book-makers' fixed odds, and firms competed only at the margins, in ante-post markets and via special offers. There was no serious price competition – the vast majority of bets were struck at starting price, a price which was the same in all betting shops.

SPs were based on the prices ruling in the on-course market. As long as this system produced margins satisfactory to the off-course industry, it was acceptable. Betting exchanges threatened to disrupt it.

In January 2003 David Harding, Hills' chief executive, told an industry seminar: "Some racecourse markets now return overrounds of only 1.2 to 1.3 per cent per runner. That is not sustainable. I cannot have a price mechanism for 50 per cent of my business being desecrated."

The desecrating culprit was Betfair, and its use by racecourse bookmakers. "If you track the overround per runner over the last 12 months," said Harding, "you can track it from the point where Betfair and Flutter merged.

"Since then, there has been a steady decline in the theoretical overround per runner."

Racecourse bookmakers were backing horses at inflated prices on the exchanges, then offering shorter prices on-course, but prices longer than those that would have ruled in an exchange-free market.

Harding's answer was for the Levy Board to force the National Joint Pitch Council to enforce rules which allegedly prohibited on-course bookmakers from using the exchanges. The Levy Board's failure to do so was "a complete abdication of responsibility".

To the big bookmakers' annoyance, Levy Board chairman Robert Hughes used his casting vote to approve a change in the rules explicitly granting racecourse bookmakers permission to bet with exchanges. Hughes explained: "The Board and its independent members are anxious to ensure that punters are protected and get the best deal. We want an open, free, fair and competitive market."

Racing's leaders, as well as the book-makers, were unhappy because, under the new gross profits based system, levy income was tied to bookmakers' profits. Smaller margins might mean smaller levy payments.

Jim Furlong, president of the Racehorse Owners' Association, concerned at the future of prize money, claimed: "The root of the problem lies with the exchanges. If allowed to continue on the current basis of operation, they will see us all in penury." Penury has yet to arrive.

While the exchanges insisted that they were not the cause of reduced margins, the major bookmakers continued to insist that they were. In February 2005 Tom Kelly, the Association of British Bookmakers' chief executive, claimed that the Levy Board's decision to allow racecourse book-makers to hedge with exchanges had contributed significantly to the fall in average SP overrounds per runner, from 2.2 per cent in October 2002 to the current figure of 1.5 per cent.

What was at issue was a more open and competitive market, one in which prices would be driven down and turnover up, but bookmakers complained that the new com-petition was unfair competition, and repeatedly made statements conveying the impression that the exchanges were not paying either tax or levy.

According to John O'Reilly, one of Ladbrokes' senior executives, "If off-course bookmakers were not required to pay ten per cent of their horseracing gross profits in levy and 15 per cent of gross profits in tax to the Exchequer or, vice versa, and the exchanges were required to follow suit, a level playing field would be created and the exchange debate would slip silently by. Level the playing field economically and the objections to exchanges just disappear."

Two years later, in 2005, Kelly claimed that if exchanges were taxed and levied on

Ladbrokes' CE Chris Bell: "I believe one race a day is fixed"

the same basis as bookmakers, in 2003/4 Betfair would have paid £45 million in gross profits tax and £18 million in levy, instead of the £9.3 million and £3.9 million it did pay – the latter towards a levy total of £100 million.

This was a remarkable claim, since Betfair's gross profit was only £49.1 million compared with Hill's £511.1 million. Although the two figures are not strictly comparable, if justice demanded that Betfair pay £18 million in levy, how much should Hills have paid?

The bookmakers' argument was based on the assertion that any exchange customer laying a horse was a bookmaker and should be taxed and levied as such, an assertion not accepted by the government.

Speaking in 2002 John Brown, Hills' chairman, said: "The law is quite clear that if you take bets either occasionally or regularly then you need a bookmaker's permit." Layers on the exchanges were acting as illegal bookmakers and Brown urged the government to take action, but the government declined the invitation.

In May 2003 the Department for Culture, Media and Sport declared: "It is not necessary for any exchange users to be licensed. There will be no requirement to license the users of betting exchanges. We regard this step as unnecessary for the achievement of the government's regulatory objectives."

Clive Hawkswood, head of the betting and racing team at the DCMS, stated, bluntly: "I can't see a situation where exchanges are going to be outlawed, and I can't see a situation where individual layers will be licensed. There is a lot of bluff and bluster and commercial vested interests."

In 2004, campaigners succeeded in persuading the Joint Committee on the draft Gambling Bill to recommend the compulsory registration of 'non-recreational' layers but the government did not adopt the recommendation, partly because of the difficulties of definition.

A few months earlier, when BHB chairman Peter Savill called on the government to set up an independent commission of inquiry into exchanges, that proposal was also rejected. The DCMS insisted that all the major issues had already been thoroughly examined.

The accusations became extreme, almost hysterical. Savill complained that exchanges had "enfranchised over 30 million people in Britain to make money out of horses losing races," while Chris Bell, Ladbrokes' chief executive, appeared on BBC2's Money Programme 'The Battle of the Bookies' to declare: "I am personally convinced that at least a race a day, if not more, is now being corrupted by the availability of laying horses to lose on betting exchanges."

Bell failed to produce any evidence and the programme left the impression of powerful vested interests, driven by com-

uncommon knowledge

miles rodgers
and the police

In 2003 the Jockey Club identified several horses owned by the Platinum Racing Club that had drifted markedly in the betting market after being laid to lose on Betfair, and did lose. They discovered that Miles Rodgers, the founding director of the Club, had placed bets through a Betfair account opened in the name of Joanne Richardson, his former girlfriend.

From 1 September 2003, racehorse owners were prohibited from laying their own horses and, in March 2004, Rodgers became the first owner to fall foul of the new rule. He was warned off for two years for having laid Uhoomagoo at Redcar and Million Percent at Wolverhampton the previous autumn.

It subsequently emerged that the account was one of Betfair's biggest, with a turnover of £4 million in 2003, and Rodgers became a significant focus of attention in a major investigation by the City of London Police.

In September 2004, Rodgers and 15 other individuals were arrested. They included Karl Burke, one of Platinum Racing Club's trainers, and three jockeys – Kieren Fallon, Fergal Lynch and Darren Williams, who had ridden many of the horses laid by Rodgers between May 2003 and March 2004.

By March 2005, a total of 27 arrests had been made, including six jockeys and two trainers. All those arrested, including Rodgers, were ultimately bailed until October and, so far, none has been charged with any offence.

For critics of betting exchanges, the seemingly ever-expanding police investigation, and other cases dealt with by the Jockey Club relating to exchange betting represented confirmation of the damage done by exchanges to racing's integrity and reputation.

For defenders of the exchanges, the cases were evidence of the effectiveness of the Jockey Club's improved security measures and of the audit trail freshly available to them.

Jockey Club and police investigations into cases of alleged fraud were not new but, in recent years, they had been characterised by failure more often than success.

It remains to be seen whether the police investigation will result in any prosecutions, or convictions, and how racing's reputation, and that of the exchanges, will emerge.

mercial self-interest, lashing out at a successful, unwanted competitor.

Yet exchanges did present legitimate integrity concerns. Betfair argued that there was nothing new in backing horses to lose, nor in those with inside information exploiting it. A horse could be opposed by backing its rivals in fixed-odds markets, or the horse sold on spread betting indices. While that was true, it was also true that exchanges offered a much easier, more straightforward method of laying a horse.

As the heated debate developed, the allegation that exchanges acted as an unprecedented inducement to skulduggery

uncommon knowledge

betfair challenged down under

Almost a quarter of Betfair's revenue comes from overseas – from punters in Australia, Asia and Europe – but the battle for international acceptance has been even more bitter than in Britain.

In Britain, legalised betting on horseracing is unusually diverse; elsewhere, bookmakers are often illegal and pool betting monopolies the norm. As threats to these lucrative monopolies edge closer, protectionist voices have become louder and more strident.

In 2002, Hong Kong banned its residents from betting on the internet and, the following year, Winfried Engelbrecht-Bresges, the Hong Kong Jockey Club's director of racing, said: "Every racing jurisdiction in the world should work with governments to ban betting exchanges. This is the biggest threat to racing's integrity and it is a worldwide threat."

The major theatre of war has been Australia, where hostility to exchanges from established racing and betting operators is intense. Betfair started taking bets from Australian customers in February 2003, an initiative that soon provoked calls for exchanges to be outlawed. Under the 2001 Interactive Gambling Act, Betfair could offer bets, apart from 'in-play' bets, from off-shore, except to residents of New South Wales, which prohibited betting with off-shore operators.

Critics of exchanges campaigned to amend the 2001 Act to make betting with exchanges illegal but, in July 2004, the federal government decided to allow individual states and territories to decide whether or not to license exchanges.

The same month, Betfair entered into a 50:50 partnership with Kerry Packer but one that was only activated if Betfair obtained a licence. Racing Victoria, Racing NSW, the Australian Racing Board and Tabcorp, Australia's biggest betting operator, have waged an anti-Betfair campaign so fierce that, in May 2005, the Australian competition authority was reported to be considering an investigation into anti-competitive behaviour.

In October 2004, ARB chairman Andrew Ramsden warned of a "strong probability" that English-trained horses would be banned from Australia if Betfair was not outlawed in the UK, while Robert Nason, Racing Victoria's chief executive, claimed that if Betfair was licensed, racing would soon be dominated by "organised crime lords. Who wants to invest in an industry that allows organised crime to flourish?" Nason advocated an international ban on English runners, to include France, the USA, Hong Kong and Japan.

At the end of 2004, the Northern Territory government announced that it would not be licensing exchanges, and Victoria recently declared that it was illegal for residents to bet with Betfair.

Tasmania has now become the focus of attention, coming under intense pressure to refuse Betfair a license. Its decision has yet to be announced.

was countered by the claim that they provided an unprecedented means of identifying wrongdoers.

In July 2002 Warwick Bartlett, chairman of the British Betting Office Association, wrote: "The problem with Betfair is that punters can go onto the website and lay horses but not reveal their identity."

Not for long. In June 2003 Betfair signed a ground-breaking Memorandum of Understanding with the Jockey Club which gave racing's regulatory authority access to individuals' betting accounts, access which Betfair's customers were required to permit.

Betfair's communications director, Mark Davies, claimed: "We have a better forensic trail than has ever existed in bookmaking, so we actually support the integrity of horseracing in a way that previously has never been possible. We have done more in three years to help the Jockey Club than the bookmaking industry has done in its entire existence." Betting shops, not Betfair, were the home of anonymous betting.

While the ABB, which later signed a more limited Memorandum of Understanding, insisted that bookmakers had always cooperated with Jockey Club investigations, the Jockey Club regarded Betfair's initiative as a major step forward.

Speaking in September 2004, Christopher Foster, the Jockey Club's executive director, made clear his frustration at the limited nature of past cooperation from bookmakers and his belief that the increased threat to integrity posed by exchanges was more than offset by the audit trail Betfair supplied.

Foster said: "By facilitating the laying of horses, exchanges have provided further and easier opportunities for people to cheat other punters. Yet the voluntary cooperation of exchanges to identify and monitor betting patterns of particular accounts has proved an invaluable tool to the regulator in investigating alleged malpractice and bringing corrupters to account.

"The most effective deterrent to malpractice comes from demonstrating that there is a likelihood of being caught. The record of success prior to the emergence of betting exchanges in catching betting-related cheating was poor. I am hopeful

uncommon knowledge

aussie papers on the attack

If Australian bookmakers are anti-gambling they certainly have the nation's press on their side judging by some of the coverage Betfair have received. Most tabloids in the UK can be expected to sensationalise stories, but Sydney's *Herald Sun* really took the biscuit when reporting on a Betfair settling error on Australia's version of Pop Idol in November 2004.

The market was being monitored in Queensland, which is an hour behind the other eastern states so the winner, Casey Donovan, had already been announced an hour before Betfair suspended. Some Queenslanders, not aware of the time delay in programming, backed loser Anthony Callea at as low as evens, but not to the extent that the *Herald Sun* would have its readers believe.

These are a few excerpts from the *Herald Sun*'s front page report:
"Victorian punters have cleaned up on Australian Idol after gamblers watching a delayed interstate telecast continued to bet for an hour after the winner was declared.

"Local punters on controversial British internet betting exchange Betfair could not believe their luck when fellow gamblers placed thousands of dollars on Anthony Callea after he had already lost to Casey Donovan. 'Basil', a Melbourne punter who did not want to be named, said he could hardly believe it when money continued to be placed on Callea.

"The punter, who made several hundred dollars by accepting late night interstate bets, said he felt uncomfortable but could not resist 'money for nothing'.

"One punter, offering even money Anthony, collected $50,000 after punters swooped on the odds."

The truth?

'It was a mistake but the sums being talked about are nonsense,' says Betfair founder Andrew Black.

"There were about seven bets placed and all but one, which was for a few hundred dollars, was for the minimum stake of $2. And everyone who lost out was refunded within a couple of hours."

That's what you call fair reporting!

---

that now the integrity of racing will, over time, be enhanced."

Racehorse owners, trainers and stable staff had already been banned from laying horses they owned or cared for and, at the end of 2004, the ban was extended to people who provided services to trainers, such as vets, farriers and equine dentists.

The debate still rumbles on, with a long-awaited Treasury decision on the taxation of exchanges still pending. Yet exchanges are now a firmly established part of the betting landscape, whose position will be formalised under the Gambling Commission's regulatory regime.

There is limited mileage left in condemning exchanges as mediums of corruption because those responsible for protecting horseracing's integrity are satisfied that the appropriate response is to establish improved security measures, with Betfair's audit trail a cornerstone.

Betting exchanges may not be good for their competitors but they are certainly good for punters, for racing – within four years of its creation, Betfair's levy payments were already 60 per cent of those made by the Tote – and for the British economy. ■

no price is too big or too small for some punters

A WORLD OF CRAZY NUMBERS

AVOGRADO'S NUMBER IS THE

By PAUL KEALY

number of molecules found in 2.016 grams of hydrogen gas (or any other gas) and its value is placed at $6.0221367*10^{23}$.

The Planck time is the time it would take a photon travelling at the speed of light to cover a distance equal to the Planck length, which is the smallest measurement of distance of any meaning. This is the quantum time, the smallest measurement of time with any meaning and it is equal to 10^{-43} seconds.

Don't worry if you don't understand a word of what you have just read. Nor do I. I just thought I'd use the above to illustrate the fact that there are numbers out there that most of us can never hope to comprehend. Some incredibly big, others ludicrously small.

The extremes of numbers that you have to deal with as an exchange player are far more limited, but it seems that lots of punters find many of those equally difficult to understand.

Neal Lancaster cost a single 1.01 punter £50,000 in 2002

How else can you explain the fact that backers at 1.01 are losing money in the long run, or that horses/dogs/sportsmen can be backed at 1,000 (999-1) and win?

Those are the two extremes – 1.01 and 1,000. You cannot back or lay at any shorter than 1.01, but you can lay and back at 1,000.

Why anyone would want to lay out £100 to win just £1 is beyond many punters, but believe it or not more money is traded at long odds-on than at any other price. You only have to look at the average American golf tournament to see how much. The winner has hundreds of thousands matched at 1.01, 1.02, 1.03, 1.04, and so on – but sometimes so does the loser.

One of the more striking examples of this came in 2002 when Neal Lancaster blew a two-shot lead on the final hole of the Canadian Open. He needed only a five at the par-four last to win by a stroke but despite being in the middle of the fairway after his tee shot, hit long and left with his second and then three-putted on the green to let

Justin Leonard and eventual winner John Rollins back into the tournament for a play-off.

Was he a genuine 1-100 chance? Someone certainly thought so, as one individual punter blew more than £50,000 at 1.01. All in pursuit of £500.

There are also countless examples in football of when a team holds a one-goal lead only to see their opponents equalise in injury time. *Racing Post* football guru Kevin Pullein has stated many times before that it can't be much more than 33-1 for a goal to be scored in any named minute but it doesn't stop the 1.01 brigade from stepping in at the death.

Early in 2004, thanks to Betfair's cooperation, I was able to complete a study of 1.01 shots over a three-month period. The period chosen was October-December 2003 and it threw up some remarkable figures.

For a start, the average number of 1.01 trades available per day was an astonishing 27 – on December 21, there were 42 individual 1.01 shots backed/laid.

The amount staked over the three months was almost £36m and, most amazingly of all, the backers lost money overall.

Based on £36m stakes, the losses amounted to just over £200,000, which is barely over half of one per cent of the total outlay. That's not a great deal given the initial sums that were wagered, but now look at it from the layers' point of view.

Having laid £36m at 1.01, their total risk was just £360,000, so a return of £200,000 represents almost 56 per cent profit on stakes, which any professional punter would tell you is a phenomenal figure.

And yet if anything the clamour for betting at long odds-on has increased in pretty much the same proportion that Betfair has grown – and Betfair is now at least twice the size that it was by the end of 2003.

At the *Racing Post* we often carry reports

the magic of McCoy

 mini marvel at Exeter

Mini Sensation's staying handicap chase win at Exeter in December 2004 proved expensive for one layer who, seeing that Tony McCoy was hard to a work just to keep his mount in touch on the first circuit, laid £8.50 at 1,000.

But he should have been aware that the Jonjo O'Neil-trained chaser is renowned for being a difficult ride and the fact he was shoved along for the full four miles of the Axminster Carpets Devon Marathon was entirely predictable. He was a long way behind, but the irrepressible McCoy kept rowing, and as his rivals' stamina began to give out, Mini Sensation's kicked in and the horse ended up winning going away.

of the astounding market moves in sporting events as well as horseracing, but now we have almost reached the time when a 1.01 loser is considered a boring story. Almost, but not quite, because the figures involved never cease to amaze and we haven't even got to the 999-1 winners yet.

And these are becoming more commonplace as well. Why you would want to offer someone 1,000 is again hard for most of us to comprehend, but it happens every day.

The winners do not occur so often, but when they do, they are likely to be very painful for the layer.

It is hard to imagine how someone could back a 1.01 loser or lay a 1,000 winner, and the immediate conclusion is that greed and stupidity figure very high on the list of reasons – but there is much more to it than that.

In 2004 Betfair spokesman Mark Davis was adamant that some big-hitting pro punters were making a tidy living out of betting at 1.01.

He said: "Would I bet at that sort of price? Not with my judgement. But there are people out there who do so very successfully. These aren't guys who are just playing the numbers game, but betting with judgement and winning.

"The beauty of sport is that you can have very strong opinions – and opinions don't get much stronger than when you think something is a slam dunk – but miracles do happen."

Well they might, but the chances are that what is happening is that people are offering and accepting the wrong prices.

Punting is all about value, which means that you have to understand the numbers. Value is the most important word in betting and anyone who tells you otherwise is likely to be a big loser.

And if you are betting at long odds-on you have to be super-successful to make it pay.

So why are so many losers being backed at such short odds? For the answer you have to understand the dynamics of exchange betting as well as simply accept that there are some seriously bad judges around with more money than sense.

With in-running exchange betting it really is a case of fastest finger first.

The sooner you get your bet on to the system, the more chance you have of getting it matched. But because everyone else is trying to do the same, there has developed a trend where punters ask for shorter and shorter prices in the hope of getting matched at bigger ones.

For instance, let's say 3 is the available price on screen to £200 about the leader going into the final furlong of a race.

Now let's say that just four punters (in reality there will be many more) have decided it represents great value and try to get on. One asks for 3, another requests 2.5, the third 1.8 and the last 1.01. If all confirm their bets simultaneously, the punter asking for 1.01 will get his bet laid first. Having asked for the lowest price, he will jump to the front of the queue.

But the problem with that hypothetical example is not only that many others will be trying the same but that the potential layers also have the option to cancel their offers. On racing, there is a one-second time delay before bets are matched, but cancelling a bet can be processed immediately.

This leads to people asking for a lower price than they want in order to get a higher one, but often being matched at their original request – and therefore taking a price that they would never have dreamt of accepting if that was all that was on offer in the first place. Even though they asked for it!

It sounds confusing but does happen all the time. I always draw the line at evens (2 on Betfair) but have still had some

Iffraaj bursts clear of Beckermet in the 2005 Wokingham Handicap

pretty hopeless in-running wagers myself. On one occasion I asked for 2 about a horse on offer at 25, and got done at 2.02 about an animal that never got within five lengths of the lead.

And a better example comes from the Wokingham Handicap at Royal Ascot at York in June 2005.

Hot favourite Iffraaj burst clear two furlongs out and was never in danger of defeat, as his *Racing Post* form comment 'readily' would suggest. But as Iffraaj was making his winning run another horse, the Roger Fisher-trained Beckermet, was also beginning to finish with some purpose.

Anyone who watches a rerun of the race will be satisfied that at no stage was Beckermet ever going to catch the winner – the winning distance was two lengths – but that did not stop the three-year-old being matched at 1.32 in-running.

Whether ante-post Iffraaj backers were covering themselves on the only danger to their bet or it was a case of serious bad judgement is unclear (the latter is far more plausible) but the fact remains a horse that could not win unless the one in front fell over on the flat was backed at 1-3.

That is just one example, but the truth is you could find a new one – several in fact – every single day. I'm sure there are a plenty of big winners who make their money by backing in-running, but it seems apparent that there is value to be had in laying as in the heat of the moment punters are forcing horses down to prices far shorter than their true market value.

Explaining away the 1.01 losers and 1,000 winners in other sports is more difficult as there is usually much more time for punters to weigh up the odds.

First of all we must accept – no matter how strange it may seem – that there are genuine cases when 1.01 backers (and even 1,000 layers) are just unlucky. There are occasions when a 1.01 chance represents value and still gets beat, with Milan only drawing from 3-0 up against Liverpool in the 2005 Champions League final being an obvious example. It does happen.

And we shouldn't be too disparaging about long odds-on players anyway as they are arguably the most important players on an exchange. Without them decent hedging opportunities would not exist.

If Betfair are to be believed, and there is no reason to doubt them, then there are genuine winners who play at the shortest odds imaginable. Fair play to them, but there must also be hatfuls of punters out there who are losing – or have lost – thousands by making bad wagers in pursuit of a pittance in return.

And this must simply boil down to a failure to understand the odds. The mentality of a lot of betting shop punters can be used as an example. Many shop punters will consider that a 6-4 favourite in a ten-runner race has a right to win and when it doesn't they will openly discuss with each other how crooked the jockey/trainer/sport

in general is. What they won't acknowledge is that a price of 6-4 (even ignoring a
bookmaker's built-in profit margin) means
that their bet actually had a 60 per cent
chance of losing in the first place.

So if some punters believe a 6-4 chance
has a right to win, imagine what they would
think of a 1-10 chance. There comes a
point when certain people think something
is so certain to win they will step in at
whatever price is available – they think
they are picking up free money.

Yet because the risks to your bank are so
big when betting at long odds-on, it is
arguable you need to be even more skilful
to make money in such a fashion. Make one
mistake and you need to find a truckload of
winners just to get your money back.

Contrary to what people might think,
backing big odds-on shots is not a mug's
game. It's just that many mugs seem to
do it. ■

the curse of commentators

LET YOUR EYES GUIDE YOU

IN AN IDEAL WORLD THERE By PAUL KEALY
would be no wars, no famine, no racism, no
natural disasters – and sports commentators wouldn't talk complete nonsense.

The emergence of betting exchanges
means our punting thrills come thick and
fast throughout the course of any sporting
event you care to mention. Other firms
offer in-running betting, but on exchanges
you are merely a click of a mouse away
from a punt – you don't have to bother with
a telephone call only to find that the price
you have seen on teletext has quickly disappeared as your bookmaker has had the
time to re-evaluate the market.

That's the beauty of exchange punting
in-running. The prices are there in front of
you – all you need to do is be quick enough
to grab them.

Yet I have lost count of the number of
times punters have been rushed into rank
bad bets simply because a commentator
has got carried away by the excitement of
the occasion or has simply made a terrible
call.

Everyone gets fed up when a race caller

tries to make a finish appear exciting when most of us can see that the horse in second is never going to get up, but you will be amazed by how many punters, taking a commentator's words as gospel rather than using their own eyes, can be talked into parting with their money at ridiculously short prices.

If you doubt the ability of commentators to have an effect on the betting market, I suggest you watch either BBC or Channel 4 before the start of a race while also keeping an eye on the market moves on Betfair. Virtually every runner being discussed and given a positive mention by any member of the two racing teams will briefly shorten, with most then drifting back out to their original price.

Despite the wealth of information around, many punters seem to want to be told what to bet on, and the need to be guided appears to continue throughout the course of whatever betting heat takes their fancy.

The following are just a handful examples of how commentators can inadvertently trick punters into placing poor-value, losing wagers. I've chosen different sports, if only to prove that all mikesmiths can be as bad as each other!

One of the most astounding examples of commentators influencing betting patterns in racing came in the Agfa Hurdle at Sandown in February 2005.

First some background to the race. The Agfa Hurdle is regarded as one of the last Champion Hurdle trials of the season, and as such usually attracts a small but select field.

And that was pretty much true of the 2005 running, with the exception of Cool Roxy, a runner rated officially 37lb below the top-rated contender – the 2003 Champion Hurdle hero Rooster Booster – according to the handicapper.

With six runners going to post, there was always a danger that a farcical tactical

Self Defense (right) collars the grey Rooster Booster at the last in the 2005 Agfa Hurdle

battle would ensue, particularly with 4-5 favourite Rooster Booster known to be in need of a very fast pace. The popular grey had attempted to make the running on his two previous starts but had failed to last home, and when jockey Richard Johnson decided to hold on to him this time, Cool Roxy, ridden by a 5lb claimer not permitted to take off his allowance due to the value of the race, was gifted an enormous lead.

At this point many punters, aided by the normally excellent Simon Holt, took leave of their senses. Remember first of all that Cool Roxy, beaten off a handicap mark of 128 on his previous outing, was rated not far off three stone inferior (approximately 42 lengths) to the best horse in the field, was 100-1 in the betting ring at Sandown and freely available at 300 on Betfair. It had no discernible chance.

Now, though, having been handed a healthy start, Cool Roxy suddenly became a serious contender, at least in the eyes of Holt and the punters who followed him

uncommon
knowledge

consistent offenders

You may think that occurrences like this are rare, and that it's a case of once bitten, twice shy for losing exchange punters, but the truth is in-running bettors make the same mistakes time and time again.

Take the end result of the Agfa Hurdle, in which Self Defense beat Rooster Booster by three lengths. It is well known that Rooster Booster was a horse with a high cruising speed who tended to find little off the bridle. The Agfa was his eighth consecutive defeat since his Champion Hurdle win in March 2003. Yet in six of those races he was backed at odds-on in-running, once at 1.01 (1-100), and most other times at 1.2 (1-5) or shorter. Some people never learn.

over a cliff by constantly asking for shorter and shorter prices in-running on Betfair.

As Holt first wondered whether the other jockeys had given Cool Roxy "too much rope" the first requests came in for the previously unconsidered beast at 100, then 80, then 60 and so on. And by the time they had entered the back straight, with the Alan Blackmore-trained runner 50 lengths clear and Holt appearing certain that it had not gone off too fast, the serious money started to flood in, first at 14, then 12, then 10 until this absolute no-hoper was matched to several thousand pounds at 6 and quite a few hundred at 5.

Imagine it for a moment. With barely half of a two-mile race completed punters were falling all over themselves to back a horse at 4-1 that they would not have considered at 75 times that price pre-race. And all this happened before the runners had entered the Sandown straight, an unforgiving climb of half a mile with two flights of hurdles to negotiate.

Those who took the 4-1 soon knew their fate, as the field closed up rapidly turning for home and Cool Roxy was headed before the penultimate hurdle, eventually coming home last, some 44 lengths behind the winner.

First of all it should be noted that you can very often back a known front-runner pre-race and then lay it at shorter prices once they are off, and many traders may well have been contributing to the bandwagon effect by taking the big early prices and then offering shorter ones back.

However, it is hard not to come to the conclusion that lots of gullible punters lost wads of cash by falling for a commentators' attempt to make the presence of a front-running no-hoper appear interesting.

We would all like to think we go through life without making mistakes, but none of us ever do and commentators are no exception. They routinely get jockeys' colours

Michael Sprott is given the verdict over Danny Williams

mixed up (not surprising given there are so many similar colours to sort out), call the wrong horses home, incorrectly name fallers, etc, and every time they do, someone somewhere makes the mistake of believing what they are hearing, rather than what they are seeing.

Developing your own idea of what is happening rather than blithely accepting what you are told is essential to in-running punting, and is just as pertinent in sports outside of racing.

To illustrate this point in *The Definitive Guide to Betting on Sport*, I highlighted a particular boxing contest between Shane Mosley and Oscar De La Hoya, in which Ian Darke was constantly blinded by De La Hoya's skill and failed to notice eventual winner Mosley's best efforts, so I'll use a different example here if only to show how often these things happen.

British title contests are unique because only the referee scores the fight compared to three individual judges under all world organisations. Just how fair this is is open to question, especially given the ending of the fight between Danny Williams and Michael Sprott.

Their 2004 British heavyweight title clash was an interesting betting heat as Williams had been a controversial winner of both their previous encounters. He was quite a strong favourite with the bookmakers and exchanges alike, and continued to be on Betfair throughout the course of the bout.

But it was surprising how strong a favourite he was considering that the bout was a truly awful contest, with very little action and far too much preening and showboating from Williams. Indeed, it was far from crystal clear that the champion was building up the sort of lead that the Sky commentary team believed.

Williams controlled the fight in the early rounds, keeping Sprott at bay with his jab and landing with some looping upper-cuts.

But the underdog never looked in trouble and wobbled Williams with a right-left combination in the seventh and again with a left hook in the eighth as the champion switched off.

Throughout the bout referee Dave Parris gave Williams several warnings (although he stopped short of docking points) about his persistent play-acting. However, the Brixton man continued right up until the closing bell.

In fairness to the Sky commentary team, it was hard to argue with their assessment that Williams was the best man on the night (albeit not by as much as they reckoned), but neither they nor Williams seemed to take into account the importance of the referee.

If you are in a closely-contested fight the last thing you want to do is cheese off the only man who decides who wins and loses, and after seeing Parris' obvious frustration throughout the 12 rounds, it was not unreasonable to expect he would lean towards the man who hadn't been irritating him all night. That appears to be what happened, with Parris walking straight over to Sprott and raising his hand, much to the chagrin of Betfair punters who were still wading into Williams at 1.1 after the final bell.

Thanks to Betfair, you can bet in-running on virtually all sports nowadays and even the more obscure disciplines get the treatment from punters when there are no other major events to compete with.

The number of people who normally bet on athletics is probably miniscule, largely due to the lack of options (although Stan James offer a decent service throughout the summer), so it was surprising to see that that almost £2m was matched on Betfair's Olympic women's marathon in 2004.

To most sports punters there is nothing less interesting than watching a load of women you have never heard of pounding the streets, but the 26-miler in Athens had a guaranteed British audience thanks to the presence of hot favourite Paula Radcliffe.

The other reason punters were so drawn to the race was because once it had reached the halfway mark it became apparent that there were only two genuine gold medal possibles remaining. They didn't include Radcliffe, who was clearly struggling in the oppressive heat and gave up some way from home.

Narrow any betting event down to only two possible winners and you have a perfect market for trading, especially when there are plenty of betting fluctuations, and people who made serious money on this race have Brendan Foster to thank for calling it gloriously wrong from start to finish.

The race itself boiled down to a match between Mizuki Noguchi and Catherine Ndereba, although it wasn't really a match at all.

Noguchi took a clear lead after around an hour and 40 minutes, at which stage she

taking it on
the chin

 responsibility lies with you

Don't go making the mistake of believing that that a commentator's cock-up gives you the right to absolve yourself of blame for a poor bet. It doesn't. With the exception of horse racing, not a single sport was designed with betting in mind and the vast majority of commentators have little or no interest in the punting habits of their viewers. And nor should they.

All the examples given here involve bad calls, but a commentator's responsibility is to make interesting a sporting event, and it could be argued that if they got it right all the time that coverage would be so much duller. By calling something wrong, they can give an event the appearance of an element of surprise, where it doesn't really exist.

Remember that with all betting, you are the person parting with your money and you alone are responsible.

was briefly matched at 1.5. Yet Foster was continually bothered by her habit of looking at her watch and wandering off a true line as she did so. He was convinced that Ndereba was running more fluently and repeatedly said it was only a matter of time before she closed the gap, which was around 70 metres.

I was totally convinced by Foster, a former European 5,000m champion and twice a world record-holder at 3,000m, and about as respected as you can be in British athletics.

I just thank my lucky stars that I was sitting on the floor playing Junior Monopoly with my son rather than punting at a computer because I am pretty certain I would have ended up in dire straits.

Yet many people must have been swayed by Foster's commentary because Noguchi constantly traded as the outsider of two in-running even though her lead of 70 metres or more was never significantly reduced.

Indeed, the Japanese girl, still miles clear, was being backed at 2-1 at 6.22pm on that Sunday afternoon, and crossed the winning line less than five minutes later with the lead intact.

Having watched the race and digested the betting information afterwards, it is impossible to come to any other conclusion than that Foster had single-handedly distorted the market to such an effect that a genuine long odds-on chance – some would say nailed-on certainty – was allowed to trade at odds-against just moments before the line.

The final example is nothing to do with commentators but still goes to show that far too many punters are happy to believe what they are told rather than what they can see with their own eyes.

The 2005 World Snooker Championship final between Shaun Murphy and Matthew Stevens was tightly poised at 5-3 to Stevens and Murphy looked highly likely to reduce the deficit to just one frame when he took a 53-15 lead in frame nine.

While Murphy was eyeing up a tricky (though, it has to be said, not desperately hard) red, the BBC's on-screen scoring graphic announced that the Rotherham youngster was 38 ahead with 35 remaining, meaning Stevens needed a snooker.

This immediately led to punters falling over themselves to back Murphy in the frame nine market with £4,000 matched at 1.02 and £1,500 at 1.01.

The BBC had got it wrong, though, and anybody with half a brain and the tiniest degree of snooker knowledge should have spotted it.

There were actually two reds left on the table, which meant there were 43 points available. You could have forgiven punters for wading in had one of the reds been out of picture, but the reality was that they were quite close to each other, so with Murphy homing in on one of them, you couldn't miss the other. To be fair, Murphy was clearly long odds-on to win the frame, but never in a million years was he 1-50 let alone 1-100. He missed and lost the frame to a Stevens clearance.

What you have read are just a few examples, but there are enough to write a book about on their own and the whole point about this chapter is to warn you that when you are betting in-running you are on your own.

If you think you know your sport – and if you don't you are playing with fire anyway – your opinion is as good as that of anyone else. When you are trading in-running on TV sport, everything that is happening is unfolding in front of your eyes – it's your call.

If you allow yourself to be swayed by people who have no regard for the betting element of the sport, you will, on occasions, find yourself in a dreadful position.

We all get frustrated at times when we believe a commentator is talking complete nonsense, but thanks to Betfair you no longer need to resort to throwing bricks at your TV. Simply log on to a computer and start backing your opinion against the sheep incapable of forming one by themselves.

Maybe these guys aren't such a bad thing after all. ▪

amazing betting stories

STRANGER THINGS HAVE HAPPENED

ALL PUNTERS HAVE THEIR FAVOURITE betting stories. They might be about the life-changing win or the agonising near miss. And they could even be about the moment of madness that suckered you into a monstrously bad value bet.

Not many people like to talk about those, but the chances are most of us have fallen victim at some stage. And the beauty of exchange betting, on Betfair at least, is that all betting moves are transparent. Right up until a market has been settled you can look up the price history of any selection you like and see how much money has been traded and at what price.

You might not know who struck the daftest bet of all time – there are many contenders but the person who backed Terry Venables at evens to get the Spurs manager's job in 2004 and then watched El Tel drift out to 100 within a couple of

By PAUL KEALY

hours will know he's a candidate – but you will know that someone has.

This chapter is devoted to some of the weirder things that have happened to the exchange punter over the last few years – although it's only a small selection as rarely a day goes by without something amazing happening.

Some will serve to remind you that greed and stupidity will always claim their victims in the end, others will show that there really is no such thing as a good thing – 1.01 losers do happen, as do 999-1 winners even if they should be 4,999-1 – and, hopefully, others still will make you burst your sides at just how remarkably, incredibly, incalculably idiotic some people can be. There really is one born every minute.

And this brings us nicely to subject number one.

DON'T DREDGE THIS ONE UP AGAIN

That's what this punter would undoubtedly say if he had the courage to confide in his mates about a bet that is going to embarrass him for life. He didn't speak to his pals, but he did come clean to me after calling the *Racing Post* in a desperate bid to see if he could recover any of his money.

This is both a sad and funny story – with about an 80-20 split in favour of funny.

At the start of his third round in the 2003 Madeira Island Open, up-and-coming Welsh golfer Bradley Dredge had the perfect possible start, a birdie three taking him into the lead in an event not covered live on TV.

However, on the European Tour website Dredge's name disappeared off the leaderboard and dropped to second-to-last. The website had mistakenly put him down for a 30 – 26 over par for one hole.

What happened next still takes some believing. Dredge began to drift in the betting from being one of the market leaders at around 4-1. And the drift showed no sign of abating until the Welshman was matched at 500 (499-1) on Betfair.

It took a few minutes for the European Tour – and the BBC who carried the same misinformation on Ceefax – to correct the error, but the damage was done. At the very best, someone had struck the daftest bet of his life (others had of course secured amazing value), while at worst, this could go on to cost them a fortune.

And the bad news for layers is that Dredge went on to play the round of his life, equalling the European Tour record of 60 on his way to an eight-stroke lead, which he comfortably converted into victory the following day.

The aftermath was one of the funniest things I have ever come across in betting, with one particular punter threatening to go to the police and sue the European Tour in order to get his money back. This, you see, was somebody else's fault, not his.

He would never have been stupid enough to believe that a professional golfer could take 30 on a single hole unless a source as reputable as the European Tour had told him. And he didn't hear any alarm bells ringing despite that fact that Dredge was in second-last position on the website's leaderboard ahead of a player who had just been credited with a 40!

"I've got a big decision to make, but I'm not ruling out getting solicitors or the police involved," whined the 42-year-old, who was both angry and embarrassed by his situation. So much so that he asked us not to name him in the following day's *Racing Post*.

"At the very least I want europeantour.com to admit misinforming people and compensate me for their mistake."

He reckoned the website should have corrected their error much earlier than was the case and only just stopped short of accusations of impropriety.

Bradley Dredge with his Madeira Island Open trophy

"I'm not saying anything untoward has happened, but when you think about it, it would be quite easy to do. I was acting on information I presumed to be correct and it's not like I just jumped in," he said. "I thought to myself that it had to be wrong, but kept on checking on europeantour.com and BBC Ceefax and there was no correction.

"After that I spoke to a friend, who said to lay everything I could because Dredge couldn't win from there.

"Thankfully he is the only person I have told. I can't tell the rest of my friends because I'm so embarrassed about it. I must have laid around 50 bets in total and they ranged from 7-1 to 110. Basically, anything that appeared in pink I clicked on.

"I'm not normally a big punter, but I've lost £10,000 and that represents my life savings."

[For the hard-hearted of you, that was the sad bit!]

But surely it takes some believing that a golfer, even a 28-handicapper, could take 30 strokes for a single hole?

229

"Yes, with hindsight it does sound stupid," he admitted. "But when you think of it, if someone is doing a leaderboard you would imagine they would know how important the leader's score is, so how could they put up 30 and not think that something was wrong?"

To lose your life savings on a bet is a horrific lesson to learn, but there is only so far that your sympathies can stretch.

I went out and kicked a golf ball to a 400-yard hole at my local course – not when any of the members were looking – in less than 30 goes, so for someone to believe a professional golfer could take 30 when he normally needs only two to reach the green is beyond explanation.

This man was so consumed by greed that he never stopped to think.

NO JOY FOR SAMBA SUCKERS

THE World Cup qualifying match between Bolivia and Brazil in 2001 set the early running for the biggest price about a winner ever to be matched on Betfair.

It remains as strange now as it was then, largely because the price laid about Bolivia – 600 – was matched when Brazil were leading only 1-0 and there was nearly an hour left on the clock.

Edilson gave the following year's World Cup winners the lead after 26 minutes at La Paz and shortly afterwards one punter managed to get £10 at 600 on the home side. Bolivia are hardly a big name in world football, but it is reasonably well known that the country has a big advantage in home matches due to the fact that La Paz is situated 3,650 metres above sea level and most sides are not used to playing at such an altitude.

Whatever the case, Bolivia were level at half time through Lider Paz, and won 3-1 thanks to 69th and 89th-minute strikes from Julio Baldivieso.

uncommon knowledge

an historic moment of stupidity

THERE have been several cases of winners being backed at Betfair's ceiling price of 1,000 (999-1), but not after they have already won.

That's what happened on 31 January 2004, when the Toby Balding-trained Historic Place was backed/laid at 1,000 and 550 after passing the post a length to the good in the Conversation Pieces Standard National Hunt Flat Race at Ascot.

The post-race activity stemmed from a lengthy stewards' enquiry into an incident in the final furlong in which the winner had hung across runner-up Senor Sedona, and Betfair's records revealed that £3 had been matched at 1,000 and a further £15 at 550 on Historic Place.

And even though the analysis in the *Racing Post*'s results section suggested the winner was fortunate to keep the race, it also noted that racing's established reluctance to throw out the first past the post made it almost inevitable that Historic Place would keep it, which it did.

It's hard to explain how people could come up with such odds other than to say they made a simple mistake – they were possibly asking for 1,000 but hit the lay button instead.

Betfair spokesman Tony Calvin said at the time: "It's a remarkable figure to be laid and backed. Someone either had a very strong opinion or it was a bet made in error because the horse was also traded at 75 and 40.

"These things can happen in the heat of the moment when it's fastest finger first and the person hits the lay button instead of the back, but then they would have had to have the funds in their account to cover it. There is no way of telling."

THE TOP VALUE 1.01 SHOT THAT LOST Many people believe that those who bet at odds of as short as 1.01 deserve everything they get when something goes wrong. Why risk £100 for the sake of winning £1, so the argument goes. And while there is no doubt that several exchange bets are struck at far shorter odds than their true chances imply, sometimes it can be argued that 1.01 is nowhere near short enough.

By the end of 2004-05 football season there had been only two English sides since 1984 to win the European Cup.

There were no betting exchanges when Manchester United were outplayed by Bayern Munich for 89 minutes and won 2-1 thanks to two 90th-minute goals in the 1999 final, but there certainly was when Liverpool were outclassed for 114 minutes

Liverpool players celebrate their shock 2005 Champions League win

but beat Milan on penalties in a remarkable 2005 final in Istanbul.

Milan were hot favourites for European Cup glory and no-one was about to disagree when they ripped apart the Liverpool defence inside the first minute, with veteran Paolo Maldini slotting home. And things got much worse for Liverpool, who were 3-0 down at the break, a scoreline that in no way flattered Milan. Indeed, the Italians were value for much more.

The only surprise about the half-time betting moves was that only £142,000 had been matched on Milan at 1.01. The truth was, no-one else wanted to lay them. They were home and hosed.

But no-one told that to Rafa Benitez's troops, who were sparked into life when captain Steven Gerrard scored with a header on 54 minutes, while Vladimir Smicer and Xabi Alonso had levelled the scores by the 59th minute.

Liverpool were on the ropes for the rest of the match, including half an hour of extra time, but won 3-2 on penalties thanks to the heroics of keeper Jerzy Dudek. The fact that Liverpool were easily second best on the night did not matter one jot to English football supporters in general, and Liverpool fans in particular, but it certainly did to Milan's backers on Betfair.

Most people would agree that Milan should have been shorter than 1.01, so the Italian side's backers can claim to have been involved in a truly rare event. They had secured genuinely good value at 1-100 and still lost. Indeed, Liverpool had drifted out to 250 on Betfair's outright Champions League market at the same time.

IT HAD TO BE MCCOY ON FIRST 1,000 WINNER Record-breaking Tony McCoy is not the sort of rider you associate with rank outsiders but the most successful jump jockey in the history of racing made all the difference to a couple of punters who made their own mark in exchange betting history by becoming the first backers to be rewarded at odds of 999-1.

McCoy was unseated on the 8-11 favourite Family Business on the second circuit in the Feast of St Raymond Novices' Chase at Southwell in January 2002.

However, this was about to turn into one of the strangest races in the history of the sport, with all six of Family Business's rivals either falling, unseating their riders or refusing. One of them, Eaux Les Couers, has the form book comment: led to 3rd, led 10th until fell 12th, remounted, left in lead when refused and unseated rider 4 out.

McCoy's mount, which was the third of the seven runners to depart initially, was matched to £4, at 1,000, by a layer who claimed he was acting in a community spirit and by offering such a price was simply warning fellow punters that the horse was no longer in the race.

But when everything else was put out of the contest, McCoy ran back out on to the course, remounted Family Business and

Tony McCoy record Betfair's first 1,000 winner on Family Business

came home alone in a time rated five minutes outside the *Racing Post* standard.

A lengthy stewards' enquiry ensued, but, much to the chagrin of the Betfair layer, the result stood. The layer still tried vainly to get his money back, but eventually accepted his fate, saying: 'Under Betfair rules I am happy for the bet to be honoured, but you can be sure I will not be alerting other users about fallers in the future.'

Was this a punter with noble intentions or just a greedy layer coming unstuck?

It's long odds-on he was the latter as you will see plenty of horses trading every day at 1,000 – some for some serious money after they have fallen. One of the problems is that the pictures watched by a lot of punters on, for instance, At The Races are a few seconds behind those of SIS.

Then again, the 1,000 layers also provide a service to the smaller layers, who may wish to pay a small charge to free up funds so they can bet on the next race. Let's say for instance, that a punter has laid an even £250 of Family Business and his liability represents his total Betfair balance. He may wish to have a bet in the next race but can't do so without depositing any more money as the race won't be settled in time. If he places £2 on Family Business he wipes out his liability and his £250 is now free to be put to use elsewhere.

This is why you will often see several hundred pounds matched on guaranteed losers.

OOPS! WRONG MARKET We've seen from the opening story about the Bradley Dredge backer that there can be no limit to a punter's greed and that was certainly the case during the 2002 Tour de France when one Betfair player's attempt to mop up some easy money could have seriously backfired.

The credit for this story must go to the often entertaining and informative Betfair chatroom (beware, like most anonymous chatrooms it is also full of racists, sexists and conspiracy theorists, plus, of course, losers eager to find someone to blame) and the user who goes under the pseudonym of Mr Knowitall.

We'll let him pick up the story from the thread he posted.

"Someone, spotting the ONCE team had won today's team time trial, backed every penny of ONCE (including a few hundred at 1.01) and then laid every other team for whatever was there.

"Unfortunately for the greedy so-and-so, he or she did it in the wrong market, namely the Overall Team category. If you need a laugh, have a look at the price histories for ibanesto.com, Rabobank or CSC Tiscali. ibanesto (laid at 1,000) is the best one, as a major Austrian bookie that prices up everything on the Tour has them at 3.5 second favourites tonight."

The day after this happened, ONCE were trading at around 1.72 on Betfair for the overall team classification, and thank-

uncommon knowledge

£2k simply swept away

We have to bear in mind that not all exchange users are based in the UK, but even so I find it hard to believe there is a genuine betting market for curling, that curious game in which one team member slides a slab of stone towards a target, while all the rest chase after it sweeping madly with brooms.

But the World Championships in Scotland in March 2005 prove that if there is an odds-on shot to be backed or a rank outsider to be laid, some crazy soul will always be ready to accommodate you.

And that's what happened in the Paisley event when a layer's attempt to nab just two quid cost him/her almost £2,000.

The bet, at 999-1, was laid when Canada trailed Norway 10-7 at the final end of a match that would see them qualify for the play-offs in dramatic fashion. Canada's unlikely comeback stemmed from a flashed takeout by Norway's Dordi Nordby (that's how the Canadian Curling Association put it) to tie the game 10-10. And Nordby followed up with another flashed takeout to hand Canada an 11-10 victory.

For non-curling fans, unless you know what a flashed takeout is none of this is going to mean much. It seems to mean an attempt and failure to hit one of your opponents' stones out of play. This must be fairly rare given the size of the stones and it not hard to argue that the 999-1 layer was out of luck when Nordby failed twice in a row, especially when hitting any one of three when 10-7 ahead would have been enough to secure victory. Then again, staking two grand to win two quid? Would you do it?

Whether the layer was the chatroom user who goes under the pseudonym 'kitz' is open to question, but this is what he/she had to say: "The Norway squad should drive to the outskirts of Oslo, climb to the top of a high cliff and hurl themselves into a fjord."

fully for the not-so-intrepid punter, they went on to win, although not before giving him a few palpitations.

999-1 COUP ON SOUEY Even some of the daftest trades are undertaken with a bit of consideration and a modicum of knowledge about the subject in question, but that cannot be said about this one. In September 2004 Graeme Souness took over from Sir Bobby Robson at the helm of Newcastle, much to the surprise of the betting market and one punter in particular, who laid £1.50 at 999-1.

The remarkable thing about this bet is that the layer had no form to go on and could have had no inside information on

time delay delights

 bet to win a fiver that copped £47,000

It is usually considered a massive disadvantage to attempt in-running betting when your pictures are slightly behind those watched by others, but every now and then it can work in your favour.

And that certainly happened to a female Betfair punter in June 2005. The lady in question asked for £500 at 1.01 on the cruising favourite King of Foxrock approaching the third last flight in the Texas Maiden Hurdle at Navan.

However, while her At The Races screen showed the horse to be tanking along, at the time it had actually made a bad mistake, nearly ejecting jockey Ruby Walsh out of the saddle. Those with the faster pictures – either from SIS or in Ireland – overreacted to what was admittedly a serious error and the result was that the Betfair backer, who was attempting to mop up easy money at long odds-on, was matched at 95. She has Walsh to thank for a miraculous recovery as King of Foxrock went on land a life-changing win – banking £47,000.

which to act, but simply thought 'Souness for Newcastle? No chance.'

And then bet £1,500 to win £1.50.

Of course, not a single tabloid newspaper had put Souness in the frame for the post, although that is not surprising, since most of the time they get things wrong anyway. That's why you can have multiple odds-on favourites for managerial positions.

EXPENSIVE EXAMPLE OF A COMMON MISTAKE One of the first of many cock-ups I have made as an exchange user was to put the wrong figures in the 'your odds' and 'your stake' boxes. Instead of asking for a fiver at 65, I asked for £65 at five. It was a relatively cheap lesson to learn.

But that wasn't the case for one South African punter on the 2005 US Masters. Instead of placing $4 on outsider Robert Allenby at 1,000, he inadvertently asked for $1,000 at 4 – and got the shock of his life when his meticulously-assembled betting bank was swallowed up in one fell swoop.

The punter, who confessed to his horror rick on the site's forum, mourned: "I just made the biggest mistake of my life. I am a 19-year-old South African and it has taken me months getting that money."

His only consolation was that because of the way bets are matched on Betfair, he took the best $1,000 available to back on Allenby, which meant he was matched at an average of around 40. Still, Allenby was trading at 800 later in the day and failed to put up any challenge, much to the delight of one of the layers, who logged on to find out he had laid £283 about a total no-hoper at 5-1.

THE BUTLER DID IT Talking of comebacks, you will never see a more dramatic one than Kent's last-gasp victory over rivals

Ian Butler celebrates taking a wicket for Kent, but it was his surprise form as a batsman that cost some punters in 2004

Glamorgan in the Totesport League in August 2004.

Indeed, so hopeless was Kent's task, that it is surprising that anyone wanted to back them even at 1,000. However, £50 was backed at that price by one individual punter, plus many other wagers at 550 and 400. Having been set a target of 143 in a match reduced to 25 overs, relegation-threatened Kent, looked down and out at 115-9 with just two overs remaining.

They needed 28 runs to win and had to rely on pace bowler Ian Butler (one-day average of 2.25) and Robbie Joseph, whose one-day career had so far seen him produce just three runs.

Butler produced the form of his life, whacking the ball to all parts of the ground, but even then the task looked to be beyond him when the Kiwi was left requiring a six off the final ball.

However, the pressure had been mounting on Glamorgan, and bowler Adrian Dale lost his cool, sending down a full toss which

Butler gratefully smashed over the ropes.

As Betfair spokesman Tony Calvin said at the time: 'I seriously cannot recall a more unlikely win in any sport, given the previous incompetence of the Kent tailenders, and I'm not even sure if odds of 1000 do it justice.'

FOOTBALL'S FIRST 999-1 SUCCESS

It was only a quid but the person who put up £1,000 to win it will wish they hadn't as football witnessed its first 1,000 winner on Betfair in January 2005. To be fair, it must have been at least 5,000-1 that Inter would come back from a two-goal deficit in injury time against Sampdoria, but that's exactly what happened.

All three goals are listed as being in the 90th minute according to football website soccerbase.com, with Obafemi Martins starting the comeback, Christian Vieri leveling the game and Alvaro Recoba scoring the unlikeliest of winners in the fourth minute of added time.

GOLD CUP LAYERS GET A KICKING

If you want know whether a horse is going to run in a big ante-post betting race the best place to check is Betfair. If the animal in question is trading at somewhere near the high street bookmakers' prices, you can rest easy that all is well. If however, it is drifting like a barge, maybe out to a three-figure price or more, you can be equally sure that something has gone wrong and it is a non-runner.

Or can you?

It's sad but true to relate that news of injury, illness or death among racehorses appears to reach the exchanges within minutes of the occurrence. Obviously someone somewhere is getting on early as the movements in the market are generally the first sign that something is wrong.

However, it does not always go well for the layers. In March 2005 Cheltenham

Gold Cup hope Kicking King was reported by trainer Tom Taaffe as having scoped poorly a couple of weeks before the race and was effectively ruled out.

By the time Taaffe had made this announcement, word had already reached the Betfair market and Kicking King had drifted out to Betfair's ceiling price of 1,000. Unfortunately for the layers, though, the seven-year-old scoped clean a week later, worked well and was suddenly declared a starter for the Cheltenham showpiece.

The rest, as they say, is history. Kicking King romped home by five lengths as the 4-1 favourite. Some punters had backed it at 100 just to be placed.

What you have read here are just a selection of examples. This book could have been filled with them. There have been 1.01 losers in every sport you could care to think of. And if nothing else, they show just how boring betting life would be without exchanges. ▪

making use of automation

HI-TECH
BETTING

By SEB BARKER

EVEN BEFORE THE ADVENT OF exchanges, some specialist punters have sought to automate their betting. Tote and Pari-Mutuel punters in some parts of the world have had the facility to submit a batch of bets for some years before betting exchanges were invented. However, the fact that exchanges charge on net winnings (as opposed to a charge for every bet placed) gives punters the opportunity to trade – placing many bets to establish a position. Those who have spent some time trading a position manually will have asked themselves whether they could automate it.

In 2004, Betfair launched their API which not only facilitates automation of trades, but provides a range of services to read market information and data on your bets. Other exchanges have a similar facility, but this chapter will be limited to discussion of the Betfair API as, at the time of writing, it provides access to the greatest liquidity. So what is an API and how do you use it?

TECHNICAL DESCRIPTION API stands for Application Programmers Interface and is designed to allow programmers with some experience to write programs that retrieve data and place bets on the Betfair system. Betfair have chosen to use a tech-

241

nology called SOAP/web services because it provides the most generic access – allowing many different languages and operating systems to use it.

It is not actually necessary for programmers using the API to have an in-depth understanding of the technology used, as the most common languages (Java and .Net) provide tools to make it virtually invisible to the user.

Experienced programmers can program in a variety of languages. The most commonly used ones are Java and .Net (either C# or VB), although VBA/VB6, Perl, Delphi, C++ and some others are also in use. Most use libraries provided by the programming environment and Betfair also provides programming libraries to support some languages.

AUTOMATION So how can the API and betting automation help an exchange user? First, it is important to make clear that writing an automated betting program does not guarantee profits.

If you automate a poor strategy it simply means you will lose money automatically instead of having to sit at the computer all day and lose. Therefore, the first step is to devise a strategy that you think will work. Having done that, you can test the strategy, manually if possible, to see whether it works in the way you think it should.

If it does, then you can build the automation tool to actually implement it. Should this prove successful, you can profit from it, but you will need to continue monitoring its performance and analysing whether your initial assumptions are still valid. You will almost certainly need to make revisions and changes as you use the system.

Let us look at some of the strategies and some issues with their implementation. There are a number of possible strategies, but they can be divided roughly into two camps. I will term these "fundamental

uncommon knowledge

 technical terms explained

XML – Stands for eXtensible Markup Language and is analogous to the language the API speaks. In order for you to communicate successfully with someone, you both need to speak the same language (in the case of this chapter we both speak English). Similarly, your computer needs to provide XML to the Betfair servers so that Betfair can understand the request. Technically, XML is self-describing, so that it provides not only the data that you wish to transmit, but also some information on what the data relates to (metadata).

SOAP – Stands for "Simple Object Access Protocol" and provides a way of addressing the request so it reaches its intended destination. If you were sending a letter to the Betfair servers, then you would write it, put it in an envelope, address it and you may provide additional information to ensure secure delivery (eg. give it a registered delivery sticker with a serial number). In a similar way, Betfair's API servers expect a SOAP envelope that describes where it is going, provides information on where it needs to be delivered to, and verifies who you are. The envelope is a specific form of XML that conveys this information – the form of the XML is the standard protocol known as SOAP.
 In fact, the technical operation of the Betfair API does not vary from the website as much as you might think. For website access, your browser submits one of the Betfair pages with any data you have entered (this is termed "submitting a form") and Betfair's servers look up the data required to make the response page (or, in the case of a bet placement, processes the bet and gets the response from the database), creates the page – adding graphics and other text to make it readable then returns it to your browser.
 For API access, you submit a SOAP request in the same way as you would submit a web page (but to a different server). The API server will receive the SOAP request, process it, returning data from the database where necessary, and then give a SOAP-formatted response to the user. Clearly, in the case of the API, there is no need to return graphics or other text to make it more readable.
 SOAP web services are used to provide a standard way of accessing Betfair that does not depend on the layout of the website.
 Therefore, while it is possible to write programs that access Betfair, or any other exchange, by pulling data from the website itself, the program may have to be changed every time Betfair modify the market view page where the odds are kept. Programs that access the API are subject to fewer changes.

analysis" (form study) and "technical analysis" (trading on market movements and anomalies).

Many associate bots (automated trading systems) with technical analysis – trading strategies – but automation can also help form students place bets that strictly conform to their strategy. Personally, I analyse form and calculate estimated odds of the various outcomes for specific horse races. Having done this, I can use automation tools to try to obtain the best value for my selections. Using these tools also ensures that I adhere strictly to the parameters I have set – ensuring a more disciplined approach.

One example I have seen involves a spreadsheet which uses the API to look up the best prices currently available to back and lay.

This is linked to form analysis to determine what represents a good back bet and what represents a good lay bet. The user then enters an amount he is prepared to risk on the race and the spreadsheet will calculate what bets to place in order to get an equal return on all backable selections, while risking no more than the specified amount. Further inputs allow the user to specify certain selections as "savers" (break even if they win) and others as "winners" (highly profitable).

Of course, it may be that the user does not simply want to take the prices available, but to try to obtain better value by asking for bigger prices. The spreadsheet can advise of the current overround on the market and give an idea of what prices to ask for on the selections that are backable prices.

In theory, you could fully automate the form analysis and betting procedure. You would generate your probabilities for each selection, compare them to the market and then place bets where the market is out of line. However, form analysis tends not to be quite so cut and dried and often requires some other more subjective factor to be taken into account.

Few would want to trust that their specialist application will give accurate probabilities every time even when the market is wildly out of line with the predicted odds. Sometimes the market itself will provide valuable clues, perhaps about potential non-runners or players who may

uncommon
knowledge

 semi automation

Rather than running a fully-automated set, the form student may find that what suits better is a semi-automated set-up, where he can review the bets he is about to place, update or cancel before submitting them.

have an injury that is not well known. In these circumstances the punter may decide to leave well alone, or at least moderate the bet.

BUILDING A BOT The second type of strategy – technical analysis, or trading – is, perhaps, a more common form of automation. There are a number of different trading strategies employed by bots – the term 'bot' is basically short for robot, which is a program that places bets automatically according to the parameters you have laid down.

To take one common example, one type of bot will look for an overround of less than 100 per cent on the back side or greater than 100 per cent on the lay side.

Should they find such a market, they will either back or lay all selections in the hope of guaranteeing a profit. While this is only one of many strategies that can be adopted, it is one of the best known and illustrates a number of issues with bots, so is worth further discussion.

At first, this may seem like a way to make a nice, guaranteed rock-solid profit with very little risk. However, there are a number of problems.

First, as it is very common, there will be a number of bots with the same strategy. This means it becomes highly competitive. For example, you may build a bot that looks for opportunities where it can lay all runners to realise a profit of five per cent of its stakes. It will therefore look for markets which have an overround of 105 per cent.

It will probably never find any, as other bots are acting when the margins are much more slender – perhaps 102 per cent.

You may therefore have to alter the bot to look for overrounds of 101.5 per cent. However, as soon as another bot operator realises that you are operating to more slender margins, he will shorten his to perhaps 101.3 per cent. In this way the bots will come down to very tight margins very quickly and guaranteed profits will be very small in every race.

This is fine, because even if you are making only tiny profits on each event, provided you can guarantee profits, then you will still be earning on every event with a suitable overround, and will still, probably, make a reasonable return.

However, there are other factors at work which mean that these bots cannot ensure a profit. First, there is no guarantee that the market your bot sees is not going to change by the time its bets have reached the Betfair database, especially if other bots are trying to do the same thing.

Thus, your bot might see £50 available to lay a horse at 2.3, but by the time a bet gets to the market it might have been taken. In truth, the risk here is limited (for events that are not in-play). If the market is very active, it is likely that your bets will be matched shortly after they have been placed, even if the bot is not quick enough to take the price that is there.

This is due to the natural activity of the market where bets on most selections are being placed very frequently, so bets at around the market price are likely to be matched. If the market is not very active, then the bets you want will not be taken down or matched by others very quickly, so the bot is likely to be quick enough to take advantage.

A more serious issue that can jeopardise guaranteed profits is the effect of non-runners. If, for example, you lay all tennis players for Wimbledon to guarantee a profit no matter which one wins, you are making the implicit assumption that you will receive the stakes from all lay bets on all competitors apart from the winner. However, if a fancied runner is withdrawn, then current Betfair rules state that the bet is voided and you will have to pay out

uncommon knowledge

keep track of rules

Other factors to bear in mind when operating a bot strategy targeting overrounds would be the number of possible winners on the market and the number of winners that have already been settled. In the Premiership relegation market, there are three 'winners' so you will need to work to an overround of 300 per cent not 100 per cent. However, if Fulham get relegated with five weeks to go, then they will be settled as a 'winner' and the market will remain open, so the overround you should work to is then is 200 per cent. This is not necessarily apparent from the information provided in the API.

on the winner at full odds without receiving the stakes gambled on the withdrawn runner. This could leave your bot significantly at risk. In fact, a number of markets may trade over 100 per cent on the lay side for this very reason.

The situation in horseracing is a little better, because you will benefit from a reduction factor on the odds of other horses when a non-runner is removed. However, if the reduction factor is out of line with the market, then a bot can be significantly exposed. Therefore you must first be careful to choose the right markets to play on and, if you decide to play horseracing markets, then you should build in some protection when reduction factors are a long way removed from the odds.

So, from a comparatively simple strategy, you will have to determine a number of business rules and exceptions that need to be catered for if you are to implement a successful trading bot. This type of detail is typically the difference between a winning and losing bot. It is relatively easy to produce a bot which wins most of the time, but gets caught out occasionally and blows a month's winnings every now and again. It is much harder to catch all the exceptions and avoid that one losing race.

The strategy outlined here is a well-trodden path and is unlikely to make you a fortune if you attempt to replicate it. However, the mechanics of technical trading on an exchange are still being developed and new winning strategies are emerging all the time.

Some strategies examine the state of the market – where the money is now and where it has previously been matched – and make bets based on a predicted market direction. For example, if there is a lot of money to back a certain selection that remains unmatched, it might be reasonable to suppose that the selection's price might contract. If that is the case, you could back it now, hoping to lay off at a shorter price later and guarantee a profit.

BEATING THE BOTS Before I move on to discuss third party tools and software, let us look at the benefits provided by automated trading systems to exchange users who do not use them – how do you beat the bots?

Remember we said earlier that a bot is only as good as the strategy it implements. A bot implementing a poor strategy can and does lose. Given the amount of automated trading systems on the modern exchange, it is unsurprising that some give opportunities to get the best price on your selection, or sometimes to lock in a profit.

For example, if you are interested in backing a selection in a market featuring several heavily-backed runners (perhaps 99 per cent on the lay side and 105 per cent on the back side), then you can entice the overround bots to lay you a price by offering to back your selection at a price that pushes the overround on the lay side to 101 per cent. A bot will then be happy to fill your price, together with others on the market, giving you the best price on your selection.

The "best-price" bots can be exploited, particularly in quiet markets. If you find yourself awake at 3am with nothing better to do, try a few experiments on quiet markets. Lay a selection on a UK horseracing market at just above the current price. Wait for a minute of two and you will probably find that a bet will appear in front of yours. If it does, then you can be pretty confident that at least one "best-price" bot is operating on the market. There is often more than one, which will help your cause.

In order to exploit these bots, it helps to have an idea of which selections are overpriced – if the *Racing Post* has too big a price on your fancied selection, then so much the better. Early morning, the market will be betting to large overrounds, but there can still be some selections which are decent value.

Don't put offers up to back your selection; some bots take notice of this and withdraw their offers to lay. You can normally put up a fairly small lay bet at the best price and the bots will often beat it.

Wait before taking the price, as another bot may come in and beat that. If not, try moving your offer ahead of the bot's. You can test to see how far you can push it. Once you have got it to go as far as it will, then you can back your selection. Of course, generally you will only get small amounts on, but sometimes there can be quite reasonable sums available. Don't forget to take down your original lay bet. Once you have your back bet on, put up an offer to back on at a lower price.

The bots will quite often beat that, giving you the opportunity to lock in a profit. This may seem a little strange as you would think bots would not want to lock in a loss, but, in truth, you are probably playing one bot off against another.

This method can be used successfully to get the best price or get a little extra value on a market. This works particularly well if you have a clear idea of what price you want and even better if you are anticipating a market move.

However, clearly there are risks involved in putting up lay bets where you actually want to back a selection. It is also likely that bots which get caught this way will be revised to ensure that they do not lay a price quite so easily. Any bot that can be easily exploited on its own will naturally have a limited lifespan.

THIRD PARTY APPLICATIONS As well as enabling bots, Betfair's API has enabled numerous interfaces to be constructed so that you no longer need to place all your bets through the Betfair website.

At the time of writing there are more than 20 applications commercially available, and a number of developers who will build bespoke interfaces.

To date, the most successful of these have been mobile applications, which allow users to access Betfair on the move. Betfair has not built an interface that works on a Java-enabled phone, but the API has allowed third party developers to fill the gap. These are now available fairly cheaply from two or three software vendors.

Betfair has always to be aware that the website is the first view that new users will get of Betfair and adding greater degrees of sophistication can put off the novice. However, there are a number of more sophisticated applications now appearing in the marketplace. There are some very impressive applications that have features such as enabling you to view and trade on multiple markets, simultaneously placing offsetting back and lay bets, place bets conditional on market conditions, and many others.

Like bots, commercially available products cannot guarantee profits. If they could, then everyone would get one and no-one would need ever work again. However, if used as part of an overall strategy then they can be very helpful and save a lot of work.

The question that is always worth asking when you are betting is: what do I know that other people don't? When you can come up with a good answer, then these tools can help you get the most out of your edge. ■

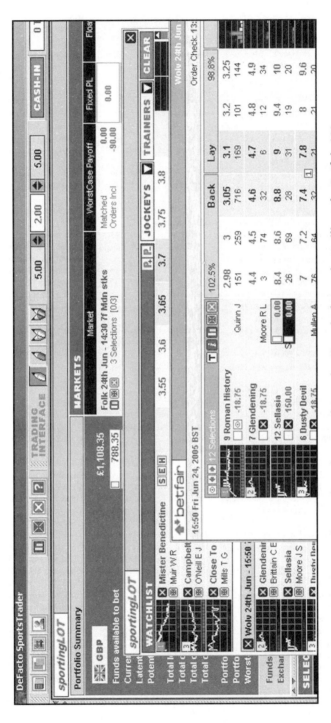

De Facto SportsTrader is one of a number of new exchange betting platforms that utilises the Betfair API

INDEX

Page numbers in *italics* refer to illustrations.